Look What God Has Done

My Journey and Faith Story

Patricia Jane Stover

Table of Contents

Dedication

First and foremost, this book is dedicated to the glory of the Lord. Secondly, this is for my precious children and granddaughter, Wesley Jane Tuck Harrison, Brooke Kathryn Harrison and Phillip Joseph Tuck, and all related spiritual children, both young and old. It is for all who inspired, encouraged, supported, prayed with and for me and believed in me, like Ann Haines Vandeventer, Leah Sedwick Pack, Missy Hubers Phillips and Linda Eggelston Hubard. And for the Reverend Vivian Utz and sons James and Joe, Daniel Ingram, the Rev. Dr. Franklin Gillis, Wenda Singer, my sister Carolyn and brother Ed for the way they love me—and many more.

It is also for Jessica Johnson and all the Jessica's out there. As we worked together toward her baptism and church membership, I often shared my experiences with her. Like a hungry child, she kept returning for more. One day she said, "I wish your stories were in a book where I could read them again." And she made a fist as if grasping something. "It encourages me so. Why don't you write a book?" she asked.

Several months later my college roommate, Ann and husband Jim Vandeventer visited. Before she left, she said to me once again as she had many times, "When are you going to write your book?" Not long after, my former Pastor, mentor and friend, the Rev. Dr. Franklin Gillis said the same thing! He even suggested a few titles.

"Is that you God?" I asked.

If *I* ever was to write a book, *I* wanted it to be a scholarly and respectable endeavor, joyfully embraced in the ivory towers of the academia or a novel or book of poems that would garner the world's respect. Yes, I dreamed of writing an Annie Dillard book, so poetic and deep it would transport the reader away to the world one experiences in Pulitzer Prize winning books. But alas, again, I must be obedient. God wants what I have to give. Perhaps in these pages someone will be transported to the highest of places, to the place of the highest honor--into a close, personal, intimate relationship with the Lord. After all, that is my passion—to see persons find their way to the exhilarating freedom of relationship with Jesus our Lord. Therefore, this book is for you too! It is *not* written to the Universe, it is written to the God who created the Universe. So, humbly I offer this book to the glory of God.

We all have a story to tell that someone needs to hear. This is my story. As I write, I realize this is my testimony, my witness. I pray this encourages you to tell your story. We all "…have a story to tell to the nations…"! Go and tell it!

Acknowledgements

It is with a grateful heart that I thank my Pastor, mentor, and friend, The Reverend Dr. Franklin Gillis, who has offered guidance, moral support, wisdom, and encouragement almost from the day we met, when he accepted the appointment that no one wanted, and moved to Bon Air United Methodist Church in the late 1980s. He is retired but continues to minister to many of us. I am indebted to him for being all of these to me, and now I add one more gift he has shared with me by taking a great deal of time to help with editing. Thank you, Franklin!

Further, I am grateful for my Editor, Liam Garcia, to my friend, mentee and reader, Helen Simpson, and to readers, Carol Justis and Ella Crockett.

"AND BY THE WORD OF THEIR TESTIMONY"

Revelation 12:11

Introduction

Luke 24:13-35

After Jesus' death on the cross, two disciples are on the road to Emmaus, away from Jerusalem and all that took place there when they encounter a stranger...whom they only recognize is Jesus when he breaks bread with them.

Emmaus is where we go to make ourselves forget the world holds nothing sacred (So the world thinks!). Then the Lord meets us on the road to Emmaus, he comes in unfamiliar ways, when we least expect it. It happens in unplanned, sacred moments.

Consider the parable of the rich man and Lazarus (Luke 16:19-31). Both, the Emmaus encounter and Lazarus story, pivot at the table celebration. The story is of a rich man dressed in the most expensive clothes and enjoying the best money can buy. At the gate to his estate, a beggar named Lazarus, laid covered with sores due to malnutrition, and he longed to eat the crumbs that fell from the rich man's table. The beggar died and angels carried him to father Abraham's side in heaven. The rich man died too, and found himself in hell where he was in torment. The rich man looked up and could see far away Abraham and Lazarus. So, the rich man asked father Abraham to send Lazarus to dip his finger in water for him to cool his tongue and the agony of the fire he was in. Abraham reminds the rich man that in life he had good things while Lazarus had bad things. And now, Lazarus is comforted while the rich man is in agony. In other words, their fortunes had switched. Abraham also tells the rich man there is a barrier, an abyss, between them which no one can cross.

Then the rich man asks father Abraham to send Lazarus to his father's home to warn his five brothers of the torment to come if they do not change their behavior and attitudes. Abraham tells him they have Moses and the Prophets "…let them listen to them." The rich man objects and says they will listen if someone from the dead comes to them and they will be sorry, repent and change their ways. Verse 31: "If they do not listen to Moses and the Prophets, they will not be convinced even if someone rises from the dead," responded Father Abraham.

The story is sad, but true!

What happens at the table? Fantasize, what might the rich man discover if he shared bread with Lazarus? God's presence is elusive, fleeting, dancing at the edge of our awareness and perception. "How do you hold a moonbeam in your hand? How do you pin a wave upon the sand?"[1]

Spiritual experience is, generally, only treasured in retrospect, "Did not our hearts burn within us…" the two disciples asked after their encounter with Jesus at the table. (Luke 24:32) In these experiences, we never see God's face, but we see the backside of God. It is such experiences I intend to share with you. As I look back, I often think of many of these times as an occasion where I see God's "fingerprints" all over the experience or at times, it was obvious as the experience unfolded that it was the Lord acting on my or our behalf.

It is important to recall meeting God in the past as well as the present: "Remember how he told you when you were still in Galilee…?" the angels asked the women who had come to Jesus' tomb. And the angels spoke Jesus' words, "The Son of Man must be delivered into the hands of sinful men, be crucified and on the third day be raised again." (Luke 24:6-8) "…then they remembered."

---

[1] From the "Sound of Music," originally released in 1959.

Experiencing God is not a private gift.

Experiencing God is never for us alone! Like the discovery of the empty tomb and the command from Jesus, "go and tell" and the women immediately go and joyfully share their experience with others---*thus realities are transformed!!*

Marvin J. Besteman, *My Journey to Heaven,* Todd Burpo, *Heaven is for Real,* Don Piper, *90 Minutes in Heaven,* Bill Wiese, *23 Minutes in Hell,* Briege Mckenna, O.W.C., *Miracles Do Happen,* and others were given incredible blessings through seeing and experiencing the supernatural or other kingdoms, normally unseen by us, but no less real than what our earthly eyes see. This testament is shared because Jesus told us to go and tell others about what we have seen and experienced that they too may know, see with spiritual eyes and be blessed as well. If you are not familiar with the above books, I encourage you to read them! You will indeed be blessed.

Easter transformed reality as the world understands it. Further, Easter was not over at sundown. It stretches into the rest of our lives and forward in time. We can't call back the angels or meet a stranger again. Capturing the meaning of Easter is transforming and our lives are never the same. Transformation is an extension of Easter day reality: The risen Lord meets us on the road to Emmaus, on our daily journey. In the study of Scripture we find our heart's strangely warmed! We especially recognize His presence in the breaking of bread.[2]

This is a powerful story testament! How can we *not* go and tell and share the joy?

---

[2] Based on notes from class in Duke University Divinity School.

Will Anyone Believe...

Like many persons who consider themselves followers of Jesus Christ, I struggled with sharing my story this way. I readily shared in Bible studies, in messages from the pulpit, in committee meetings, and confirmation classes (for the baptized and to be baptized), with close friends, and members of our prayer team. But I struggled mightily with the thought of sharing through the written media! Will anyone who does not really know me believe my experiences?

Ego and fear continue to get in the way of obedience to all disciples' main mission *"to go and tell."* That mission also means to live *love*. I felt I had a ton of love bottled up, afraid to let it out. I considered myself a mother first and a scientist second. I was a research biochemist at several institutions, Phillip Morris research biochemistry unit, the Medical College of Virginia, research in microbiology and human genetics (now Virginia Commonwealth University Medical Center/Hospital) and A.H. Robins research biochemistry unit. I wrote and presented several research papers at seminars that were attended by scientists from around the East coast and Company executives. Dr. Mary Catherine Spann, Philip Morris Biochemistry Unit and Dr. Charles Dawson, head of the Department of Biochemistry at Columbia University in New York mentored me, and Dr. Dawson attended the first seminar and granted me the equivalence of a Master of Science degree following the presentation. I share this in hope that you will better understand my struggle and the ambitions that I had to give up to the Lord's will. The "old self had to die" and a new self was born.

The Awakening

These words had great impact on me from Professor Dr. David McKain, Virginia Commonwealth University: *"Somewhere I read that fear is an emotion we use to distract ourselves from knowing the truth, a kind of deliberate confusion we create to protect ourselves from whatever it is we don't have the strength to face.*"[3]

The mundane chore of taking out the trash turned into an extraordinary moment in time. It was a sunny spring day. The bird's songs from the trees lifted my spirit. I tried to practice "stop and smell the roses" in spite of the busyness as a mom, wife, church volunteer and scientist. So, I walked over to a fuchsia azalea bush so full of blooms you could not see a green leaf. Suddenly, it was as if I could see every cell in the flowers, as if a powerful microscope was taking me to the very molecular level, to the very life surging there, moving, effervescing and eradiating white light with great depth and energy! It was other worldly. I was mesmerized. As suddenly as it started, it was over and there were the...now extraordinary blooms that I understood in a new way!

These words barely describe what I saw, and words fail us in moments like these, sacred moments! This experience was not shared with anyone until recently. Why? Because it took me a long time to understand what happened and why it happened. And I thought anyone hearing the story would think I was hallucinating or crazy. I understand now in that moment God opened my spiritual eyes. I know what I saw was real! I glimpsed "the unseen." *That was my burning bush* encounter. It was a spiritual experience similar to Moses' when God spoke to him from the burning bush that did not burn.[4] It was an awakening. God opening me again to the supernatural spiritual realm of reality that I knew when I was a child. (We all know this when we are children.) Experts and scholars say that around the age of 12 we are closed to seeing into the spiritual realm and to the memories from before we were on earth. Again, they say until that age or stage of

---

[3] McKain, David, *Spellbound, Growing Up in God's Country,* The University of Georgia Press, Athens and London, 1988, p. 5.

[4] In Exodus 3, Moses, who is living in exile from his people, Israel, who live in slavery in Egypt, hears God speak to him from a burning bush that does not burn, is not consumed. From this encounter with God, Moses is sent back to Egypt to free his people from bondage.

maturation, we not only remember, but we see into the spiritual world.[5] My own experience supports the above.

A few years ago, a cousin and a childhood friend asked if I remembered seeing angels around my bed one night. I thought that was interesting. I had no recall of seeing angels, but I have a clear memory of feeling their protective and comforting presence!

Annie Dillard in her Pulitzer Prize winning book, *Pilgrim at Tinker Creek,* said it best, "in that moment it was as if I was lifted and struck like a bell." That's how I remember her words which have resonated in my mind and spirit for more than forty years! I was indeed lifted that day when my spiritual eyes were opened again and I was changed. I began to see life, all life differently, opened to new realities.

"Now faith is being sure of what we hope for and certain of what we do not see." Hebrews 11:1 (NIV): These words resonate powerfully with the experiences shared throughout my story!

Again, Disciples are to go and tell! Revelation 12:11 reminds us: "They triumphed over him [the accuser of the followers of Jesus the Christ] by the blood of the Lamb and by the word of their testimony." Through hearing and reading other people's testimonies and stories we can receive and even enhance our faith, or our faith increases, is strengthened. I can tell you from personal experience this is so. Mark Batterson in his book, *Draw the Circle, The 40 Day Prayer Challenge,* writes: "If God did it for them, He might just do it for me." I agree with Batterson that maybe this is why Revelation 12:11 puts great emphases on sharing testimonies. I am convinced this is why the enemy wants us to keep our testimonies silent.[6]

---

[5] One researcher found that over 90% of the children studied, clearly had seen angels. (From my notes of a talk given by Judith MacNutt.)
[6] Batterson, Mark, *Draw the Circle, The 40 Day Prayer Challenge,* Zondervan, 2012, p.176.

Fear and ego prevented me from sharing. Then, there is this thing I've come to also know as "God's timing."

PART I:

FAITH

Is a gift from God that is nurtured by those

around us and by Holy Spirit.

Chapter 1

In the Beginning

"Now faith is being sure of what we hope for and certain of what we do not see."

Hebrews 11:1 *NIV*

From the bay window seat, my brother and I watched the snowfall and the hustle and bustle across the road at our grandfather's and dad's country store and flour mill, Spring Creek Roller Mill. As the aroma of baking bread, cake, and pie mixed with our home's atmosphere, we excitedly awaited Dad's return from work. These memories evoke a sense of love-filled grace and the communion of relationships between families, church members, and the Lord.

In the same atmosphere, I learned to love and feel secure about whatever lay beyond that bay window. For instance, feeding the chickens their small stones or grit, and grain or gathering eggs wasn't a chore; I just loved it! Sometimes, my brother and I would lie on the grass and giggle while looking at the clouds, imagining creatures and people. Other times, we would play by the bank of Spring Creek, challenging each other to get the most skips from a rock. Then, at dusk, we would run barefoot in the cool grass, chasing fireflies—we also called them "lightning bugs."

However, most days, our mother and grandmother would sit with us and read Bible stories. As they read, vivid images of an action movie would form in my head. We always prayed before meals and at bedtime. Then, as I would retire to bed, hoping to fall asleep, the light from grandmother's room softened the black night as I drifted to sleep while listening to her loud whisper as she read from her Bible.

I suspect others might have thought I was a strange child. I loved our little Church. It was just a few doors away across the street. There, I was proud to see my Dad teaching the men's class—as our little class often got out before they were finished—and Mom taught the children's class.

I say that I was strange because I was so aware of the Lord's presence. I thought of the Lord as being everywhere. The Lord was in command of the wind and rain, everything! And I enjoyed thinking of others or at least striving to be thoughtful, and if I did not talk to or about the Lord out loud, God's presence was most often in my thoughts. And the year my brother, who is fifteen months older and was my closest friend and playmate, went off to school, I struggled with the pain of loneliness and boredom. It was awful. In the struggle, I grew more aware of the Lord's presence, so much so that Jesus became my invisible friend and playmate. A few years later, I was alone playing with my dolls when Dad came by the door to my room, stood for a moment and then went downstairs. At the dinner table, he asked, "Where did you learn that gibberish? And who were you talking to as you played with your doll?" I responded, "I was talking to Jesus." This puzzled me for many years until, during a prayer team meeting, I realized I might have been speaking in tongues that day!

My family moved to the Waynesboro area of Virginia when I was five. When I was eight, my family moved to the city of Harrisonburg, Virginia. I'll never forget my first weeks at the new school. Somehow, when I entered the building, I knew where everything was! I was familiar with the place—where I had never been! I saw faces I knew…somehow. Then one day in the cafeteria, I saw a cute, dark-haired, dark-eyed boy and the dreams all came flooding back to me. I had dreamed about these people and the school building before we moved there! No wonder there was no adjustment time for me in this new place! My folks had, on occasion, shared a dream or premonition that guided their actions and decisions. I then saw how God was caring for and guiding me and my family.

It was Labor Day vacation week, and we traveled to Norfolk and Portsmouth, Virginia, to visit family and friends. On the drive home, Dad pulled over to the side of the road because he was troubled.

"Louise," he said, "I have a strong premonition or feeling that I can't shake. I think we will have a car wreck someplace further on up the road."

Mom, in surprise, said, "I had a vision of us having a wreck! Maybe we should look for a motel for the night."

Dad replied, "I was thinking the same thing, but it seems like a waste since we are so close to home."

Mother replied, "I agree. It does seem foolish to do that when we only have maybe another four hours, and we'll be home."

Dad responded, "Yes, we can be home before too late."

So they dropped the motel idea. Around dusk, it began to rain. We were in Dad's sister's Packard with a rumble seat, and my brother and I were happily riding there. Of course, when the rain started, Dad stopped and made us join them in the cabin of the car.

It was dark. The mountain curve was sharp. The road was wet and slick, and the other car was going too fast. We crashed head-on! A horror movie became a reality when the State Trooper put the flashlight on Mom. Blood was streaming in all directions over her face. She had struck the rearview mirror, which likely kept her from going through the windshield. I was asleep but got thrown into the front seat resulting in three sore knots on my head. My brother's face

4

smashed into the clock on the dashboard, so he did not look too great himself. Dad appeared to be unhurt except for a broken bone in his hand. Mom had braced herself and thus suffered a broken arm, ankle and leg just below the knee. She was hospitalized until Christmas Eve. The State Trooper said my brother, Eddie, and I would have been thrown over the mountainside if we had stayed in the rumble seat! In fact, the car was right at the edge of going down the mountainside. Mom would have gone through the windshield if she had not braced herself and thus hit the mirror. As I see it, the rain was a double blessing from heaven that day--and Packards were sturdily built.

In this new City, Harrisonburg, Asbury United Methodist Church was within walking distance again, but a bit of a hike! My folks drove us to worship and other activities and meetings they attended. Like the Mailman, we went through snow and rain, at which our Roman Catholic neighbors marveled. We walked to youth group when my parents were no longer the leaders; how I looked forward to the Wednesday evening fellowship and all the good food! And when Mom and Dad went to choir practice, Eddie and I would explore the huge building. We found a secret narrow staircase from the second floor to the basement, a great place to play. I remember the feeling of reverence and awe that came over me when we entered the sanctuary, and the beauty of the stained-glass windows glowing from the light of the streetlamps made it seem otherworldly, holy. Mom and Dad served in positions of leadership, and Grandmother was always in the Church kitchen while Aunt Madge managed to find time after teaching five days a week to volunteer in the Church office and meet with the prayer group. At the time, I did not fully appreciate the fact that Aunt Madge and both Grandmothers kept me, us, covered with prayer. I know those prayers are still being answered.

In my teen years, like many teens, we balked at attending worship and sometimes youth meetings, but Dad would hear none of it! Often, quite disgruntled, we went off to Sunday school, worship and youth meetings because Dad made us go. In later years, I gave thanks (and still do) to wise and committed parents who knew what was *most* important for their children's growth and future.

Prayer was a regular part of our family life, and I remember often falling asleep while I prayed, which is like sleeping in the arms of the Lord. And we had family devotions for a time. Dad insisted we be at the table for devotions. That discipline fell apart when my brother had football practice, and I had to go to my job after school at Leggett's Department Store. The hunger within was fed by those times, and I devoured the *Guideposts* magazines when they arrived. My folks were avid readers, and even though I struggled with dyslexia (not diagnosed until my early 30's), I followed suit. They did not just read the Bible, they studied Scripture, and so I began delving into mine. I had a King James Version given by the Church when we "graduated" from the third-grade class. However, there were times when my frustration level became too much for me, and I began to slip off to read my parents Revised Standard Version or their Living Bible. There were times when I read the King James where I found the sentence syntax confounding and odd, while at the same time, the words in old English with the "sayeth, thee and thou," among other odd words, caused me to struggle to grasp the meaning. I would read a section over and over and still not be sure of the meaning. This contributed to feelings of being "dumb." There were sections I clearly understood, but again the strange syntax and unusual word choices just about sent me up the wall or the Bible out the window! I am so grateful for Contemporary translations. However, I am now wondering if we haven't reached the point of too many English translations. I must have close to 15 versions in my personal library. That is hyperbole; I just counted 9. (Jesus used hyperbole. Which means we exaggerate to make or emphasize a point.)

Rural churches today still have services called Revivals. Every year, the Church had a time of "revival" with a guest preacher. At first, those early "Revivals" were for two weeks, then they became one week. Today they might go from Wednesday or Thursday through Sunday. Whenever they were held, our family would be there every night.

For me, the revival during the year I was fourteen was significant. For several nights I felt like I was holding onto the pew for dear life. A strong urge to get up and go to the altar when the invitation was given for people to come forward was tough to fight! (I now understand that urge was the Holy Spirit trying to send me forward as the Holy Spirit sent Jesus into the desert after his baptism. --Matthew 4:1)

Finally, one evening I swallowed my pride and, with some dread, rose from the pew and knelt at the altar and gave myself to Christ. I had been baptized as an infant, confirmed in the faith at nine, attended every activity whenever the doors of the Church were open, and then, I found myself kneeling, committing my life again to the Lord!

From that moment until my junior year in college, I searched for what I sensed the Lord was calling me to do with my life or for an understanding of where the Holy Spirit desired me to go. Was I to be a missionary like Great Aunt Mattie Whitmore always told me? Was I to be a Christian educator like our "Jonesy" (Loretta Jones)? "What, Lord?" I asked. I searched. And whenever I sensed it was to be something *else,* I gradually developed a litany: "I'm too dumb. I couldn't possibly read out loud. My tongue gets twisted, and I lose my place. [I learned later this is because of eye spasms, lazy eye.] I could never preach! I'm a woman. Women can't be pastors! I want to get married, have children, be a scientist or be in medicine, where we save lives. I want a normal life!"

Then I thought: What on earth is a normal life? I thought I knew. I think I imagined I could have a life with a supportive, loving and faithful spouse where together we worked through relatively simple problems with a nice home and more than two perfect children.

7

Through my teen years, my faith commitment and relationship with my parents became my strength and guide as I negotiated the temptations of drinking, smoking and the lure of sex. Drugs were just beginning to enter the scene, but I never encountered that temptation. I knew alcohol lowers a person's self-control, as do drugs. Further, based on what I learned from being with my brother and his friends, who practically adopted me as a little sister, only strengthened my resolve to avoid these pitfalls. They spoke badly about the girls who were caught in the lure of sex. I had enough issues with self-esteem and knew these behaviors would take me down a dark and dangerous path from which I sensed I might never recover.

When I look back, it amazes me my classmates continued to include me in their parties and other fun activities since I refused to join in some of these behaviors…drinking alcohol, smoking or flirting with the boys!

A pivotal confrontation occurred one night at a school dance. Four or five of the guys in my class, whom I considered good friends, cornered me. I remember leaning against the cold tiled wall of the gym as they confronted me about my principles. Their nickname for me had come to me before that night, "Purity Pat." They said things like, "You think you're better than us…you're too good…Miss Pious." One of them said, "I think your middle name must be 'Purity.'"

Too many years faded the exact words of my response, but I recall the hurt I felt.

In the heat of the moment, I said, "I never look down on you! What you choose to do is your business. I respect your freedom to choose what you do. Why can't you respect me for my choice to do what I want to do? And I value the trust my parents have in me and respect my parents too much to disappoint them. If what I choose to do makes you feel bad, that's coming from you. I respect your choices, and I don't try to force you to my way. So why are you trying to force me to your way? All I ask is you respect my choices as I respect yours."

I think I also mentioned that my faith was the basis on which I made the decisions for my behavior. If I did not say so, I could tell you that besides my parents, this was the strongest motivation for my behavior. Hence the reason some called me either "Pious Pat" or "Purity Pat."

I continued to be invited to the parties, but some I could not attend because I was babysitting. When I was of age, I began to work part-time at Leggett's Department Store and continued to do so into my freshman and sophomore years in college.

During my freshman year of college, the English professor assigned a term paper. My chosen focus was to compare Catholicism and Protestantism, which came out of my faith struggle because I was "pinned" to a Catholic boy. (To be "pinned" meant you were pre-engaged—intended to become engaged.) I nearly flunked out of college because before the year was out, I had been through every book I could find about religion—Judaism, Islam, Buddhism, and more, including, of course, Catholicism and Protestantism (both are Christian)—while dealing with the strange urge to do something fulltime in ministry was the driving force behind it all. I got an A on the term paper but was no further along in obedience to the Lord or in my ability to discern what the Lord expected me to do.

During my junior year, the urge to go into ministry was intense. My litany was well developed: "Lord, I'm too dumb, I can't read out loud, I'm a woman, I want to get married, have children...." And one day, as I continued to struggle with the Lord, suddenly, I felt released, free to go my own way. And go my own way I did—yet, amazingly; the Lord blessed me.

Chapter 2

The Prodigal: The Struggle with Obesience

Luke 15:11-24

A man had two sons. The youngest son asked the father for his inheritance now. He packs his things and goes off to a far country where he spends his money on women and parties for his new friends who disappear when his money runs out. He is hungry and would gladly eat what the pigs are eating. But no one gave him any food. Finally, he came to his senses and returns home to his father who sees him from far away and runs to welcome his son home. The father throws the son a feast and party, puts fine clothes on the son. The father was thrilled because his son was lost and now is found.

I encourage you to read the whole Prodigal Son story through verse 31. For at least ten more years, I ran from the Lord's call on my life. Please understand that I believe we all are called to be in an intimate relationship with the Lord, and each of us has a personal purpose in this world. I was running from my "purpose" and trying to make the way I wanted my life to be. I was in control. I was a prodigal child. A disobedient child. I wanted God's blessings, God's protection, but I wanted to have my own way!

In the years following college and marriage, not only did I drift away from the Lord, but I seldom attended church. My husband was busy on the golf course or in a boat on weekends. And in our fourth year of marriage, we started a family. I seldom prayed. Our second child prompted us to buy a larger house on the other side of town. It was a true community. We made fast friends with many of the neighbors, those who were close in age with two or three children and those who were older with grown children. My declining health had been mostly triggered by allergies. Asthma led to pneumonia and ear infections, and back problems due to a back injury from horseback riding in the 9th grade. I also had an abdominal "tumor" removed, back surgery for a ruptured disk and several other issues that resulted in day surgery. All of these health issues were in a time span of several years. My dear mother made the comment, "Maybe God put you on your back so you would look up." She was right. I had begun to pray again.

God's call on my life began again when I joined a home Bible study group. Soon, nearly every church within reasonable driving distance found me, and sometimes my family (my husband still was a golfer and loved to fish) visited on Sundays. First, we visited a large United Methodist Church in Bon Air. Then we visited smaller ones and I visited other denominations. They just never "felt right."

One Sunday I announced, "I'm going back to that first Church, Bon Air United Methodist Church (UMC), where I felt…" I searched for the right word, "at *home!*"

Strange as it sounds that was it. I did feel at home! So off we went and after worship, somehow it seemed this was indeed where we were meant to be. My husband agreed! I think, no I *know*, this is how God called me and my family to this particular Church.

In my younger years, my family and I attended small churches with between 30 to 100 folks sitting in the pews. After the age of eight, we attended a large church with about 1700 or so members that filled the sanctuary plus the annex space for overflow. My husband grew up in a church of about the same size. By the time we found our way to Bon Air UMC, I felt like I had been off in the far country and was now back home. I had not been a part of a church for many years for some of the reasons stated above. I also struggled with

11

disillusionment with the church that *was* in relation to the church I knew we should be based on the Bible stories I had read and heard from childhood and youth years. Like many others, I thought I did not want to have anything to do with the hypocrites filling the churches. Perhaps these were only excuses, but it seemed like a real heart issue. It was. I still yearn for the church to become the church we see in the Bible's Book of Acts!

However, in spite of excuses and reasons, I began to experience a yearning, a hunger—for…something. Without question, I experienced a gnawing emptiness like the Prodigal son. So, I joined a home Bible study group, began to pray more regularly again, and got myself off to Bon Air Church. It felt like I had come home!

Chapter 3

Struggle and Conflict

"For our struggle is not against flesh and blood but against the rulers, against the authorities, against the powers of this dark world."

Ephesians 6:12 *NIV*

Other translations say *"against the rulers of this present darkness."*

"Where there is no vision, the people perish."

Proverbs 29:18 *NIV*

It was a large Church with a "small church" mentality. As noted earlier, we joined Bon Air UMC, which was a large church of 2200 members, and it was unable to meet a budget of about $90,000. It seemed to be a small budget for such a large congregation! Plagued with this problem on and off over the years, the Church was once again struggling to meet the financial needs for the Church's ministry of staff, building facility maintenance and operation, education, outreach and missions. *And* we had outgrown the building. Sunday school classes were meeting behind the stage, in the library and in every other space, including the Pastor's Study!

The nearby Baptist Church was about the same size in membership, yet their budget was about a million dollars! Those folks were no richer. Our Church was "small" in its thinking. As time revealed, the "small" thinking lacked vision which was a spiritual issue.

Then there was war. War? Yes, there was war—spiritual warfare—and we became known in our Denomination as the Church no Pastor wanted to serve! I was elected Chair of the Administrative Board. Board meetings were a challenge! On the day of the Board meetings, I took the day off from my job to pray. Honestly, I did not want to go! Whenever I had to head to the Church, I became nauseated. Tensions ran high. Smiles were scarce. Laughter was non-existent. Most Sundays, I left worship feeling down and beaten. Attendance was dropping. Rumors were that the Pastor had visited some families, and when they disagreed with him, he exploded in anger! They described their encounter as a feeling of being run over by a bulldozer. Many families began to leave to attend another church. Three groups formed: one group supported the Pastor and his agenda (which I learned after the war was to take the Church back to where it was in the 1950s, a promise the Pastor made to the five or six "big" givers in the membership); the second group opposed the Pastor; and the third, the largest group, consisted of those who refused to take sides, and thus were caught in the crossfire. The behavior and attitude of the first two groups were, "If you aren't with us, then you're against us!"

As Chair of the Administrative Board, I felt like I was walking on the cutting edge of a razor blade! I managed to stay out of the fight through constant prayer! Like a sailboat, I was constantly carefully tacking into the wind.

Then I felt something pushing me forward like a strong wind at my back. The Holy Spirit is referred to in the Bible as being like the Wind. The very sound in pronouncing the Spirit's Hebrew name is breathy, wind-like—Ru-ah (Roo-ahh). Scriptures remind us that Jesus felt the Spirit move him into the desert for his forty days of trial. (Mark 1:11-12: Jesus had just been baptized, and God the Father spoke: "You are my Son, whom I love; with you I am well pleased. At once the Spirit sent him out..." *(NIV)* And it was the Spirit that guided my heart, actions, decisions and *tongue*.

My heart ached over the negative situation in our church that was resulting in membership decline. I loved my fellow members, each and every one! Some were behaving badly. I knew the control I was able to exercise over my emotions, tongue and behavior was only possible through the strength of Holy Spirit. *(Note the absence of "the" before, Holy Spirit. That is intentional. Holy Spirit is one of three Persons of the God-head, Father, Son and Holy Spirit. It's His name. We don't say "the" Jesus, so I chose to drop the habit of "the" Holy Spirit.)*

Our Church's transition team gathered around the table. There were *twelve* of us (like Jesus' twelve disciples and the twelve tribes of Israel) representing the various groups in the Church. We discussed how to prepare for receiving the appointment of a new pastor. We discerned the direction in which the Church needed to go. Such direction would probably cause the five or six "big givers" to leave as they did not want the Church to change, nor had they liked any of the change since the 1950s! Someone commented, "The Church cannot survive financially without them!"

One of the older members prophetically responded, "Don't you see? We're building the track that the train will go over. When it's time for the train to move, there will be lots of new members who will meet the financial needs." That was early in the New Year.

In July, new spiritually strong pastoral leadership was in place. In November, new leadership was elected, except for me as Board Chair and the Lay Leader. We both were asked to continue in our office. With this new leadership team, the vision of the Church changed to "bigger." Missions and outreach would expand, mission teams would be sent out, Bible Study groups would be established, an informal

15

worship service would be added during a weeknight, the singles ministry would be started, prayer ministry would be formalized, and classes to address needs in the surrounding community would be added to weeknight opportunities. We would be intentional about bringing intergenerational groups together and reach out to persons of color and the downtrodden, single parents and the homeless!

The Church began to come within fifteen percent of meeting the budget. The budget had finally broken through the dreaded threshold and enlarged to well over the one-hundred-thousand mark. Then the leadership team decided to no longer spend days trimming the budget! The budget would be the total of what the areas of ministry requested. A breath of fresh air—Spiritual wind began to blow! The Church, finally through faith, moved to let ministry drive the budget, not the budget dictate what the ministry could or could not be!

Chapter 4

The Struggle with Obedience Continues

"We must obey God rather than men!"

Acts 5:29b NIV

The struggle with surrendering my will to God's started again when I joined the home Bible study group and ultimately found my way to Bon Air United Methodist Church. One of the first things I volunteered to assist with was Vacation Bible School. I had two young children and no elementary education training, but working with them gave me some confidence that I could do this. With the training offered by the Richmond District and lots, *lots* of preparation time, I was encouraged by the results after teaching the second graders. I discovered my favorite time of the day was the telling of Bible stories and the preparation for and leading crafts.

After a few years, someone asked me to be one of the Sunday School team of teachers for the sixth graders. My daughter was in the class, and I agreed. I prayed mightily before teaching the class. I was always amazed at what happened during class—God was indeed answering prayer! I knew the spontaneous creativity and excitement—the success of the classes all came from the Lord.

It is true! Humbly make yourself available, and God will equip you for the job. Then God receives the glory.

Eventually, I became the "resource" person to bring crafts to the sixth graders. In October, I assembled kits for the class to make

Chrismon ornaments[7] for the Church's tree. To my amazement, not only the boys but some of the dads joined their sons in class to make the Chrismon ornaments!

While teaching that class, a problem developed with one of the students. It was the "disrupter." The rest of the class paid close attention, asked good questions and responded well when I asked questions or made an assignment. But this one boy kept getting out of his seat or pestered someone near him, tossed pieces of paper about the room and generally would not follow directions. My frustration and anger toward him grew weekly. Do I "expel" him from class? Call in the Associate Pastor? His parents? I tried everything short of these drastic measures. Then it occurred to me (Holy Spirit nudging) I was not handling the situation with prayer! As I prayed for him over the next several weeks, *I was changed*. Not him. I saw him with new eyes and understanding. First, I saw him as someone's wonderful and precious child, *and* I was reminded that he was a child of God and deeply loved by his parents and God. Then I sensed I needed to make him my helper.

The following Sunday, when he entered the room, I took him aside, "Mike,"[8] I said, "I could really use your help with a few things. Are you willing to be my assistant?" He lit up, and with a big grin, he said, "Yes!"

The class experience completely changed for all of us that day. He stayed quietly in his seat and eagerly waited for my instructions. I never had another moment's problem with him.

---

[7] Chrismon ornaments are to be only white and gold made in the form of Christian symbols and objects. And there should only be Chrismon ornaments on the tree according to the group who developed these. We made crosses from pearls and gold beads. One for the child and one for the Church tree.

[8] Not his name.

God can handle any size problem, and I give God the glory for solving what seemed like a mountain.

Chapter 5

It'll Take a Miracle

"Ask and it will be given to you; seek and you will find; knock and the door will be opened to you. For everyone who asks, receives; he who seeks finds; and to him who knocks, the door will be opened."
Matthew 7:7-8 *NIV*

After much healing and numerous *Discipleship Bible Study* classes (and the departure of the five or so "big givers"), members who had left the Church began to return. There was an excitement in the air that the Church had not known in recent memory. Smiles, laughter and hugs became commonplace again. Broken relationships were reconciled. We were indeed a family! Families fight and then find their way to reconciliation because of their genuine love for each other.

With the leadership of a new Pastor, the Rev. Dr. Franklin Gillis, a visionary team was assembled—no more small thinking—and with this leadership, the members began to share their dreams with the planning committee. The new plan seemed to be an impossible *dream!* BIG PLANS were projected. They would cost *millions*! We needed to address the overcrowding condition and to have space to offer activities and address identified needs of the surrounding community to the Church. The Church's Day School also needed more space. We needed an addition to the existing building. Fortunately, we had the land needed for expansion.

The dream included a gymnasium with a locker room and showers, a suite for the bride's party and additional classrooms. Staff had expanded, so there would be the need for a new office suite. The addition of a gym would double as the new Social/Fellowship Hall, where we could seat a large attendance for activities. A large commercial kitchen and stage were projected. Covered-dish, spaghetti dinners, pancake suppers, and other fellowship gatherings would be made possible. There would be showers, lockers and a laundry area for our gym and homeless guests. The Church youth and Scout troops would have the space to expand their activities. An updated playground was planned. We wanted to invite our neighbors to come to play basketball, participate in aerobics and volleyball, and join in Bible Study and other activities.

Now understand that our Church had not been a praying Church until Pastor Gillis with some of the leaders, began to organize prayer and Bible study opportunities. This does not mean no one prayed. Some of the leaders were real prayer warriors! Worship services in the new sanctuary began to be supported by prayer teams of two in the transformed old Sanctuary, the Chapel and Parlor.

One day when I walked into the education building, it was brighter inside! I looked around for new lights and fresh paint, but no…then I realized it was the "spiritual atmosphere" of the building! The darkness had lifted. Then on Saturday, I waited at the same door for our District Superintendent, who would join the leadership for breakfast and a meeting. When Dr. Chamberlin stepped inside, he exclaimed, "Oh my!" He stopped, looked around, took a deep breath and again exclaimed, "Yes! The Holy Spirit is here!"

This change in the atmosphere was due to more intentional prayer ministry and the giant steps taken in faith. It is indeed what Paul referenced in Ephesians 6:10-12 as we struggle not against flesh and blood but against this present darkness, the forces of the spiritual realm.

Prayer soon began to address our facilities. A few months later, the leaders met in the chapel and after a special presentation of the architect's building plan, we were asked, "What will it take to make the new addition reality? Consider this question for a few minutes, then write your response on the piece of paper you received when you entered. Ushers will be around to collect your response." I prayed. Then wrote the words, "It'll take a miracle." That is all I offered. But I believed it to be a lot. As I handed my paper to the usher, I sent it off with the prayer, "Please, Lord, let the eyes that see these words may they understand it as a positive statement, not as negative or sarcasm."

I believed we could fulfill our dream for the Church, and it would happen through a miracle. Before this meeting of leaders ended, we were encouraged, "As an act of faith, you need to step out in faith and make a sacrificial pledge to the Building Fund campaign as a demonstration of leadership, the sum of which will be used to kick off the campaign with the entire membership."

To my amazement, on the launching of the Building Fund campaign, Pastor Gillis' sermon title was—can you guess? Yes! It was "It'll Take a Miracle." As he preached, he shared the vision for ministry and the miracle needed to turn into reality the dreams the congregation gave the planning committee. We needed a financial miracle. I could barely hold back the tears of joy. A miracle happened! How wonderfully our prayers were answered.

The Lord is honored and glorified when we ask for big things, even if it seems impossible to us. When the impossible is accomplished, the Lord receives the glory! A 1.2 million dollar addition was proposed for capital improvements! This was a big ask of this newly transformed Church. *(It was in the early 1990s.)*

Over the next many weeks, we continued to pray for the miracle. The Building Fund campaign would climax in a huge banquet of most of the members who would be asked to make a *sacrificial* pledge—a step out in faith. There was some anxiety regarding the outcome. All apprehension left me one day as I prayed. Every time I prayed, I visualized the "new church building," *the entire building*. On that day, as I prayed, it was as if a camera suddenly zoomed in to the very brick of one of its walls, and I was almost nose-on-brick, looking at the pockmarks and variations in color and texture. It was no longer my visualized architect's model—I was looking at *the real thing!* I instantly knew the Lord was telling us we would have our miracle!

The leadership indeed led with hundreds of thousands pledged. So, the membership responded with a total pledge that went over the top for the needed 1.2 million! As they say, the rest is history!

What changed? As the beloved, we grew spiritually. We became a prayerful Church and a Church that knew the Bible. We learned that the Bible is not just words and stories; it calls for a response and action! So, we stepped out in faith, and out of this came vision and excitement. Then the Church grew, not just in new activities, but we also grew in the number of members. We accepted the leading of Holy Spirit!

PART II:

PRAYER

Prayer is where we find our purpose and power.

Prayer, the Heart's True Home --Richard Foster

"Every time we pray, we gain a position in the spiritual realm. The kingdom of God is advanced and the forces of darkness must retreat."
Mark Batterson, Draw the Circle[9]

---

[9] Batterson, Mark, *Draw the Circle, a 40 Day Prayer Challenge,* Zondervon, 2012, p. 168

Chapter 6

Prayers

"Prayers of the righteous are powerful"

James 5:16*b;* Proverbs 15:29 *NIV*

A righteous person is one who strives to live in a relationship with the Lord. This means the person's will is God's will; they really do their best to live as Jesus taught us to live. Anyone who is in a relationship with God and continues to work to be closer to the Lord will find it not as burdensome as one might think. A truly righteous person will be humble, concerned for others, loves unconditionally and has a generous and servant spirit.

However, God chooses to answer the prayer of those we might deem anything but righteous! Jesus declared that we must become like little children if we want to enter God's Kingdom. So, the righteous trust God the way a child trusts their parent. One can only imagine how precious a child's sincere prayer of the heart must be to God. Yet, God chooses to answer the prayer of those we might deem anything but righteous.

Wesley, my daughter, was in elementary school. I was flat on my back with a ruptured disk. The next day, I was to chaperone her class on an outing and we both knew that was not likely to happen. However, I awoke the next day and felt not just fine but great. No soreness or pain!

Wesley came in that afternoon more chipper than normal.

"Hey, Mom! God answered my prayers!" she said excitedly.

"What did you pray about?" I asked.

"I asked God to heal your back tomorrow. And I asked Him to let me win the drawing for 'Milly' the class chameleon." And she presented me a small box with Milly inside then she skipped off to find the dusty aquarium stored in the attic.

"Did you ask God to heal me 'tomorrow'?" I queried.

"Yes! And he did it!" she answered.

I wondered what the next day would bring.

The next day I was back in bed, right where I had been. But I was grateful for the one-day reprieve and so very grateful for God encouraging my child's budding faith by answering her prayer!

Chapter 7

Hiding In the Big Church

God called Jonah to go to an enemy's city and preach to them about their evil behavior. Jonah did not want to go to those awful people so he hopped aboard a boat and went to the opposite side of the world from where God was sending him. He learned that you cannot run or hide from God, but first he had to be thrown overboard into an angry sea where a very large fish swallowed him. After three days in the tummy of the fish, he was spit up on shore, and Jonah went off to preach to the city of his enemies.

–my abbreviated version based on the Book of Jonah

First, I encourage you to read the whole story of Jonah, who is sometimes called "the wrong-way prophet." It is wonderful and, at times, makes you laugh. In fact, you should! I am sure the laughter of the early hearers of this story was robust. Please do not misunderstand what that might imply. Some scholars believe every word and tittle is true; others agree that it is a story to emphasize the truth about human behavior and God. My faith says God could do this if God so chose. Many of us have faith that God can do anything, and it may well be true. Yet, it does not impact one's faith if it is indeed a parody and never actually happened. It does indeed amplify the truth of human nature and behavior and of God's interaction in our lives. The Book of Jonah is rich writing indeed!

The Backstory

Did you know that a person can hide in a big church? Well, the prodigal child was now thinking like the "wrong-way prophet." I call this the "Jonah mentality," which is apparently alive and well today. I was "home" in Bon Air United Methodist Church, but I thought I could hide, stay on the outer edge of things or get lost in the crowd. Enjoy being a committee member, not a Chair, a leader. Then I came upon the idea—through prayer, and I now know it was not *my* idea— to pray daily, "Lord, make Bon Air United Methodist Church a dynamic force within this community." I must have prayed this daily for a year or more, never suspecting where "it" might lead us—or *me.*

The phone rang. It was the Associate Pastor, Katha Mills (Bollfrass today). "The Nominations Committee met last night, and we want to know if you will be the new chairperson of Church and Society," she said. Of course, I did not want to be that involved in leadership!

After a brief explanation of what this meant, I said, "I promise to pray about it."

The flesh did not want to do this, but I was growing in desire to be obedient to the Lord.

Several days later, I found myself destined to be on the Church Administrative Board as the new Church and Society Chair. You would think I had learned the lesson of being careful about what to pray. I did not want to step into leadership, but after prayer, I discerned that the Lord intended for me to say "yes." So, I became Church and Society Chair and began to develop ministries to meet needs within the congregation and the community. This position led to becoming the Council on Ministries Vice-chair and many wonderful times organizing and encouraging others to join in local ministries, missions and outreach.

I am reminded of what Mark Batterson wrote, "Don't just pray about it, do something about it." This was *one* of the lessons from this experience. [10]

---

[10] Batterson, Mark, *Draw the Circle, the 40 Day Prayer Challenge,* Zondervon, 2012, p. 159.

Chapter 8

In God's Time

"...When the time had fully come, God sent his Son..."

Galatians 4:4*a NIV*

Let me reflect again on when I agreed to Chair the Church and Society Committee. Through prayer and listening to neighbors and friends, a vision began to develop for the Church and Society activities. We began to offer evening classes, STEP Parenting classes, classes for parents with ADHD/ADD children, stress management, divorce recovery, and teen suicide. Timidly I shared the ministry vision with the current Pastor and offered to provide leadership. He listened politely, said not one word—*ever*—and without expression, walked away. The next Pastor reacted much the same way. After sharing the vision with two pastors, I was hesitant to say anything about it to the next Pastor, Dr. Franklin Gillis. However, by the time he arrived, I was no longer the Chair of Church and Society but the Administrative Board Chairperson.

Perhaps six months after Dr. Gillis' arrival, I stopped by the Church to drop off an article for the newsletter. Pastor spotted me. With the excitement of a child, he called, "Don't go anywhere." And he disappeared.

He returned with a "book" in hand and said, "Read this and let me know what you think."

Stretched across my bed, I began to read—with the proverbial lump in my throat and a tear trailing down my cheek. There was the vision spelled out in detail! We were going to do it! Excitedly I called Dr. Gillis and told him how I had shared this vision with the prior two pastors! There was much, much prayer over this Pastor's appointment, and it was clearly time, God's time, for us to finally become the Church the Lord meant us to be! The daily prayer from several years earlier, "Lord, make Bon Air UMC a dynamic force in this community," was continuing to be answered!

We advertised "Come Grow with Us" and "attend the School for Growing Christians," and of course, this included an invitation to Sunday school and worship. Looking back, it seemed that within a few years, we were almost a seven-day-a-week church, the fulfillment of the vision! And MUCH prayer was answered in God's time!

Chapter 9

This Present Darkness

"...be strong in the Lord and in his mighty power. Put on the full armor of God so that you can take your stand against the devil's schemes. For our struggle is not against flesh and blood, but against the rulers, against the authorities, against the powers of this dark world and against the spiritual forces of evil in the heavenly realms." Ephesians 6:10-12 *NIV*

It all came down—my entire world. My father died. A new Governor came into office, and the agency where I worked part-time, the agency that had the best morale (and envied by some of the other State agencies), became the agency with perhaps the lowest morale. At the same time, I finally admitted and faced the reality that my marriage was a sham. The Church—the one place where I could find peace, rest, and re-energize, was…where all hell had broken out. It was the war, spiritual warfare, as Paul clearly states, hoping to make us aware in his letter to the Ephesians.

Courage was finally found to face reality. My marriage was beyond saving and over. I admitted I was sick of the pretense and bondage. My husband finally moved out; the divorce became final on the first anniversary of filing. It was before and during this time that I was looking for full-time employment with benefits. I worked several part-time jobs with the Commonwealth of Virginia, but obviously, I needed health insurance and enough income to support my children and myself. Because of my education level and work history, the court expected more of me than part-time work provided.

I filed many job applications that resulted in discouragingly few interviews. Finally, I had an interview with the Vice President of Human Resources at Virginia Commonwealth University for a position that recognized my education and life experience. I was working hard to keep a lid on my excitement because I felt it was a position in which I could excel with the bonus of enjoying my work once again!

The Vice President of Personnel, Steve Moore, who interviewed me, was an acquaintance through my Church. The interview went great! I left with renewed hope and controlled excitement. I was certain I had a good shot at the position, or so I thought. Several days passed when my Pastor called. He informed me that following the interview, Steve called him excited. He shared that Steve said, "I've finally found her! I just interviewed Pat Tuck,[11] and I'm sure she's the one we've been looking for." Dismay does not fully describe my response.

The Pastor continued, "The Nominations Committee has been searching for several years for the 'right' woman to become the first woman Board Chair. You are the one! (The "glass ceiling" can exist in churches as well as businesses. No woman had chaired any of the "high" or executive positions in the Church.) We want you to become Vice Chair for this term with the understanding that you *will* become Administrative Board Chair," he said.

I was speechless for a few moments as the irony of the events involved in this turn of my anticipated future sunk in. Then I responded. "I need a few days to pray and consider this 'opportunity.'"

Everything in me was screaming, "NO! I don't want to do this! I need a paying job with benefits!" The flesh is strong. But I was learning to be obedient to the Lord's will for my life.

---

[11] My name when I was married.

Perhaps the normal response should be disappointment or even anger, but I laughed! God has quite a sense of humor. I interviewed for a job at Virginia Commonwealth University to support my family and myself, for a salaried position with health insurance, and to be paid for a day off, and God offered me a job to serve others without pay! Note I did not say the job God offered without pay was *not* without benefits because it did have benefits, just not what I needed physically, specifically health insurance and paid leave. However, looking back, I realize God was providing God's health insurance because I was in the longest period I ever had without being sick or needing to see a doctor.

It would be a lie if I did not confess that I wrestled mightily with this decision. "I want to be a committee member, Lord, not the Chair of the Administrative Board!" As I said in the beginning, I still wanted to be responsible for just a little, not the leader of much! This was not a small Board. An average meeting would boast 85 members present of the 100+ Board members. And what would I encounter? This Church never allowed women into this inner circle of leadership. I had become comfortable as the Church and Society Chairperson, but this?

Again, I laughed. When God first called me to ministry around the age of fourteen during the revival services, I dug in my heels and raised many reasons why I would not go. At that point, I confessed I did not want to be a barrier breaker, and I was convinced the church did not allow women to be pastors. Let someone else break such barriers. Not me! However, I was learning if God wants a person to do something, it is much easier to just admit you do not understand why God wants *you* to do it, much less how you will be able to do it! Make it easy on yourself. Beloved, give in quickly. Make yourself available with the understanding that it is God who will do whatever God wants you to do. God will equip you for the task and guide you if you just let go and trust the Lord. But I am a slow learner and hard-headed. So again, like Jacob (whom God renamed Israel) and his offspring, I struggled with God.

The Bible is full of unlikely persons being chosen and called to ministry for the Lord. For example, the original twelve disciples were humble, ordinary and uneducated! The young Mary became the Mother of Jesus, David, a young shepherd boy defeated a giant and became the King of his nation, and Cyrus, who did not know God became a pagan king. In Isaiah 44:28; 45:1, 4b-5 NIV:

The Lord "...says of Cyrus, 'He is my shepherd and will accomplish all that I please; he will say of Jerusalem, 'Let it be rebuilt,' and of the temple, 'Let its foundations be laid...' This is what the Lord says to his anointed, to Cyrus, whose right hand I take hold of to subdue nations before him...I summon you by name and bestow on you a title of honor, though you do not acknowledge me. I am the Lord, and there is no other; apart from me, there is no God. I will strengthen you, though you have not acknowledged me..." (In some translations, Cyrus is called God's "anointed".)

The list could continue of persons, who, on their own, were quite ordinary and even weak, yet God used them for God's purposes. The weak, the uneducated, too young, too old, with speech impediments and no leadership experience, and unbelievers were chosen. God led them, equipped them, and gave them strength and courage to stand up, speak up and lead, teach and above all, to love unconditionally no matter the conditions or treatment from others. We can look back in biblical history and see that God, not the person, was doing these things, and it is God who receives the glory. It is also important that the world sees that ordinary, unskilled, or weak persons could not possibly do what they have done without God's empowerment. The world can see God's work through the humble, weak and unlikely persons! God does not wait until we are worthy, equipped and qualified! God claims and calls us just as we are, warts and all!

Finally, as I prayed, "I confess, Lord, I do not understand why me, but I will do what you want me to do."

I became the first female Vice Chair of the Church Administrative Board and, several years later, the first woman Chairperson. One leader, upon hearing of my nomination, yelled at the Pastor, "I CANNOT, I WILL NOT WORK WITH A WOMAN! I resign!" Before this, we seemed to enjoy a good relationship—and not only was he a cousin of my spouse, he was a lawyer! However, he stopped speaking to me, and soon, he would not even look at me—and within the year, he found another church.

This sudden "rise to position and power" did not sit well with some others in the Church. People with whom I enjoyed a good relationship, men and women, suddenly would not smile, look at me or speak to me. I know about and experienced the proverbial "cold shoulder." Some of them actually glared at me. But I continued to speak to them and treat them as I always had. My dear mother taught me to continue to be kind and loving even in the face of someone's unkind behavior.

"Turn your enemies into friends," she counseled and "Heap hot coals on their heads," and she lived it as witnessed by her three children. So, with the Lord's help, I continued loving them and ignoring the caustic expressions and their silence. In spite of their rejection, I felt confident I was walking in the will of God and doing the Lord's work.

This experience turned out to be excellent training for my future. I was indeed learning to be obedient. The Lord commanded us to love one another as he loved us. When we do, others will know we are his followers. John 13:34-35: *"A new Command I give you: Love one another. As I have loved you, so you must love one another. By this, all [people] will know that you are my disciples if you love one another." NIV*

During this time, my husband and I separated. The part-time work was not enough to meet expenses. There were weeks when there was no money for meat and milk—and I went deeper into debt each month. I prayed for help, for financial blessings. When I succeeded in really letting go and giving it to God, positive things would happen. One of those times, my in-laws stopped by. The doorbell rang. I opened the door, and there stood my precious in-laws, Mr. and Mrs. Tuck. "Patrick[12]," Daddy Tuck said, "we were on our way to do some shopping when something just told us you could probably use this." He handed me a check. Another week, my doorbell rang, and I was surprised to find a man, who was not a Christian, standing there looking a little uncomfortable. "Hello, Pat. I have this fresh catch of fish, croaker and spot. I thought you might use them," he said. I knew from scripture that God would use anyone! Moses was a murderer. Cyrus was a pagan, as mentioned above. And I was not yet aware of how God intended to use me. I was not too fond of fish! However, that week they never tasted better, nor were they appreciated more.

---

[12] His pet name for me.

Chapter 10

God Makes A Way

As people saw the blind man which Jesus healed: "His neighbors and those who had seen him begging asked, 'Isn't this the same man who used to sit and beg?' Some claimed he was. Others said, 'No, he only looks like him. But he himself insisted, 'I am the man.'"
John 9:8-9 *NIV*

It was dark. The house seemed larger and empty. I was tired from a long day, weary with the burden and strain of taking my son to the hospital. He was depressed and suicidal. The phone rang. Irritated, I wondered, "Who is calling me now?" A voice from years ago, a college acquaintance, greeted me from the phone. I was in no mood to talk to anyone. I feel I was less than cordial. She persisted. Soon I shared that I had just put my son in the hospital—and she *laughed!* I was a split-second away from hanging up on her had she not quickly explained, "I just brought my oldest son home from the same hospital!" We began a renewed and close relationship.

"I've been back in town for a little over a year," she said. "I was looking through the current College Directory of alumni and saw you now live in the area! I intended to call numerous times, but it just occurred to me to call this evening." The timing of her phone call was really God's timing. One of God's serendipities or a coincidence which I define as one of God's little miracles!

When we talked, we learned that both of us were now divorced and struggling to find a job. Further, she had been growing in her faith and trust in the Lord. She shared some wonderful healing experiences her prayer group had while I shared some of the amazing things God had done in my life. She invited me to her prayer group numerous times. One evening, after a number of months, perhaps even a year or so more of resisting, I decided to go with her to the prayer group meeting. Again, it was in God's time.

Seated in a circle, each one introduced themselves and offered something about who they were. We sang praise songs accompanied by a guitar that was followed by Bible study and prayer. There was a woman sitting across from me who seemed familiar, but I was sure I did not know her. There was another woman I recognized as one who had attended a graduate school Master of Fine Arts class with me at Virginia Commonwealth University. However, I did not really know her.

At some point in the evening, the first woman, who seemed familiar, shared, "Last year, I was completely blind. I've had a number of operations, but the doctors told me long ago they had done everything possible. So, I was given a seeing-eye-dog and was working for the State in the Department for the Disabled. Last fall, this group laid hands on me for eight weeks at each prayer meeting. After the first time, the darkness was a little less dark. And the next week, I was sure I was seeing a little light! Each week it got brighter until I could see!" she said. "Next week, I will be getting my driver's license and will lose my job with the State."

"Why?" I asked.

"Because I'm no longer disabled. And my dog was about to be retired, so I can keep him as my companion. I'll bring him to the next meeting so you can meet Bishop."

Amazing! It was then I remembered! Excitedly I said, "I have met you! It was a year or so ago when you came to the Department of Education, Special Education, for a meeting. I received a phone call and was asked to meet someone with a seeing-eye-dog at the elevator. And they asked me to lead you to the Conference room."

Months later, I invited a man from my *Disciples Bible Study* class to join our prayer group. Julie[13], the formerly blind woman, recognized his voice immediately. He had been to her home years earlier and was a friend of her former spouse. He said to me, "No, that's not Julie. She looks something like her but it's not. It can't be!"

Both of us knew we were living the scripture from John 9. In fact, in my experience, once my eyes and mind were opened or awakened, I saw that God's word, found in the Scriptures, is repeated in our daily lives in each new generation. The age-old message of God never grows old!

My story is no "imaginary" one. It is indeed a fantastic and true story of how the Lord works among us. Some of us yearn to see the Book of Acts come alive again in our lives, here and now. Again, I assure you this is true! We knew her as a blind woman whom we did not recognize once her sight was restored. It recalled to mind the Bible story of the man Jesus healed. People were not sure it was the same man they had known who had been blind!

Often in church, we hear that the Bible is a living document whose story is repeated over and over, even into our present time. My experience reminds me of this truth! I now feel I have been led by the Lord to share my story through writing.

The prayer group meetings are a vital part of my story. During the first meeting I attended with the prayer group, I could hardly wait for break time! I wanted to talk with the woman from my graduate school

---

[13] Name changed.

class. Several months earlier, the Lord brought her to mind as I prayed. A picture of her came to mind. Every day for about a month, the Lord brought her to mind as I prayed. So, I prayed for this person whom I had not seen in years and barely knew. I confess I had not thought of her since the class ended. Now there she was! Here we were now on a faith journey together.

After my husband left, I worked two part-time jobs and sometimes three. I became frustrated with the lack of time and energy for the "hands-on ministry" I had come to enjoy while Church and Society Chair and participating in the outreach and local and international missions ministries. One night I prayed, "Please, Lord, give me a way to be involved in Your ministry again. You know the demands of my jobs and family responsibilities. There are not enough hours and energy to do more. But I yearn to be involved in Your work! Help me find a way!"

The answer to that prayer came quickly. A few evenings later, as I prepared for bed, I found myself balling, wracked with sobs. I rushed into the master bathroom and closed the door, hoping not to alarm my children. Intuitively I knew this was not my pain, not my struggle! As I continued to sob uncontrollably, I asked, "Lord, what is happening? Why am I experiencing such distress?"

Instantly I knew this was the gift of "burden sharing"[14] for my friend Katherine[15] who had remarried and moved away. "Can I call her Lord?" I asked. I heard no voice, but my spirit led me not to contact her. After maybe twenty minutes this strange phenomenon stopped. I continued for a long time to ask the Lord if I could call Katherine--but was led not to do so! I made a note of the date and time of the event for future reference.

---

[14] Galatians 6:2 *Carry each other's burdens, and in this way you will fulfill the law of Christ.* NIV
[15] Name changed.

On the way to my parents' cabin in the mountains, I stopped by Katherine's home. After we visited for a while, I finally asked, "What happened on July 7 around eight P.M." The date I recorded. Katherine stared at me. "Stunned" best describes her response. Clearly shaken, she asked, "How do you know about that?" I shared the above experience.

Then she explained, "That night, as you know, we had been married about eight months when my husband fell 'off the wagon.' I had no idea he was an alcoholic! He tried to kill me!" She explained. "Somehow, I managed to escape from the house. I ran down the street into the church building and locked myself in the office, where I called the police and waited for help."

This new ministry of burden sharing was the answer to the prayer for the Lord to help me find a way to be involved in God's ministry. One day while I was at work, I had a vision of Jerry Brown's face— actually, it was his head with a big grin, just as I remembered seeing him through high school and college when we double-dated. We never dated, but I counted him as a friend. This vision kept coming and I realized the Lord was calling me to pray for Jerry. This continued for about a year, several times a day; then it stopped as suddenly as it began. Then, I forgot about it.

In the fall of the following year, I attended a college class reunion. There was Jerry! He was the picture of health. He practically leaped over tables to come to say hello to me. I mustered the courage to share, "Jerry, for about a year, the Lord kept putting you on my mind several times a day, prompting me to pray for you. Was there anything going on you might share?"

Amazed that I asked, he replied, "I was cutting firewood with my chainsaw when it hit metal deep in the log. The saw bounced off the metal into the top of my forehead—and took it off!" he explained. "I was in a coma for months. The doctors' diagnosis was dire. My wife's church prayed hard for me, and the doctors can't believe my recovery."

There he was in front of me! Fully recovered and was as handsome as ever! I could see that his forehead looked slightly different from our youth, but he truly looked great. And there was no scar!

He added, "I always admired your faith and how it guided you. I decided one time I wanted what you had. I prayed for six weeks for that kind of faith, but nothing happened, so I gave up."

Jerry[16] and I did not stay in touch. I can only hope and pray his eyes were opened to see his prayers were answered and he found his way to the most awesome relationship and freedom with the Lord. Trust in the Lord, a real relationship with Jesus is that which this world cannot give. Our culture has developed a mentality and demand that we want and should have what we ask for quickly. Gratification now, right now! Sadly, I got the impression that six weeks of praying for faith was a long time for him. I do not think he realized prayers live on, and perhaps in God's own time, they were indeed answered.

I am often reminded of Mark Batterson's encouragement to persist in our prayer life. In counterfactual fashion, he asked, "What if Israel had circled Jericho only six times and then had given up?" The answer is the walls would never have come down. God would not have answered those six days of prayer because God told them to circle and pray for seven days. One more week of prayer, fourteen weeks of prayer. I know it would happen! I *know* from experience at times, God tests us. God sees our hearts and works to build our strength and our depth of commitment. If we are committed and sincere, we can persist!

---

[16] Real name used. Jerry has gone on to his reward.

I became accustomed to the Lord bringing to memory persons for whom I was to pray and with whom I was to burden-share. So, I prayed for the woman, who was practically a stranger from graduate school, sitting across the circle from me for my first time with the prayer group. During our break, I shared with her, "Several months ago, for about a month, the Lord brought you to my mind and so I prayed for you."

She replied, "I was facing surgery at that time. I was scared. Really scared. And thankfully, all went well, really well."

It was then I knew I was in a place and with a group the Lord had called together. I could hardly wait for the next meeting!

God Makes a Way for Me Again and Takes Care of Me

Another time God powerfully answered prayer. It was still difficult to make ends meet with the expense of graduate school at Duke Divinity School and everything else. I noticed my tires were "bald." How could I buy four new tires?

I prayed an "arrow" prayer, "Lord, please help me find enough money for those tires."

It was just before the early service and as I walked to the Church entrance, the Lay Leader came up to me concerned and said, "You've got some slick tires there. You might want to go to Collinsville Tire Service. I know they will give you a good deal."

I thanked him, but I am not sure what else I said. Then as I got out of the car at the second service, a couple came up to me and put an envelope in my hand and said, "The Lord told us you need this." I discovered the envelope contained a check for two-hundred dollars. I was amazed—again!

A day or so later, I went to the tire specialty store in Collinsville. The owner convinced me to buy four Michelin tires that would give a good ride, and they were on sale—*and* well over the amount of money I had, yet the price was about what I usually spent on tires of lesser quality. So, my VISA would take another hit, and the two-hundred dollars would go as a payment there. I took the waiting time to study in preparation for my next sermon. The owner soon came in and handed me the bill and as he did so, he noticed my Bible and inquired, "Are you preparing a Sunday School lesson?"

"No, I am studying for next Sunday's sermon."

He lit up! "You preach? Hand me that bill."

He scratched through something and then wrote somewhere else. When I looked at the revised bill, guess what he wrote? "$200!"

He looked up at me and asked, "Is that okay?"

I could not say a word—I was holding back the tears…and he said, "Uh-oh! Is there going to be a flood?" I nodded yes. When I was able to speak, I told him, "You need to understand what just happened. I had no money to replace my bald tires and asked the Lord to please help me buy new ones. Yesterday when I arrived at the second Church, a couple met me with an envelope containing a check for two-hundred dollars, saying, 'The Lord told us you need this.'"

"Don't you see how you, too, are the answer to prayer along with the couple who provided the check?" I asked. And I thanked him for his faithfulness and for being an answer to prayer.

Chapter 11

The Prayer Meetings

"And the Lord told him, 'Go to the house of Judas on Straight Street and ask for a man from Tarsus named Saul, for he is praying. In a vision he has seen a man named Ananias come and place his hands on him to restore his sight." Acts 9:11-12 *NIV*

At the next prayer meeting, there was a strong "urge" to get up and go to one of the women in the group, lay hands on her and pray. I fought the "urge" the entire prayer time. During the time we were in prayer, my hands had a strange tingling sensation, almost as if they were electrically charged. When we adjourned for the break, I immediately felt ashamed. I knew I had been disobedient to the Lord. I approached the woman and told her what I experienced.

"Well, pray for me now," she said.

Never had I laid my hands on a person while I prayed. We sometimes held hands, but this was different. Quickly and to myself, I asked, "Lord, what do I do?"

In a flash, there was a "picture," a vision of me standing behind her with my hands on either side of her head. As I prayed for her, imitating the "vision" with my hands on either side of her head, suddenly something moved down one arm and over me and then it was gone.

"Oh, I felt 'something' leave!" she exclaimed.

46

What I felt as it moved over me was "depression." "Have you been experiencing some depression, feeling down?" I asked.

"Yes. I have. But I feel like a weight has been lifted now!" She confirmed.

This does NOT mean all depression is from such a source. It's the "present darkness" that Paul writes about in Ephesians 6. Some depression is a chemical imbalance and needs medication. I have no doubt the Lord can bring the body chemistry back into balance. But this is not the type of depression she was healed of that evening. It was from the spiritual realm.

A few years later, I encountered something similar to this previous experience. Jody[17], a delightful infectious personality and former eighteen-wheeler truck driver, had health issues and needed someone to drive her to Forsyth Hospital in Winston-Salem, North Carolina, for a heart catheterization. She, in fact, had experienced a silent heart attack and did not know she had one! It was discovered during her annual check-up required by the trucking company, who immediately retired her.

Jody was very masculine. She lived with another woman, and both had moved to this conservative rural area where they were embraced by both churches and were well-loved and cared for by the members. It was beautiful to see! A group in the community offered transportation to persons who could not drive themselves to appointments or even to buy groceries. There were widows in this rural area who never learned to drive!

One day Jody called, "I need surgery and will undergo a heart catheterization next Thursday. I need someone to take me and to wait for me. I was hoping you would do this."

---

[17] Name changed

I replied, "Jody, my schedule is pretty full; there is a Committee with a list of folks willing to do this. Did you try one of them?"

"I called Sandy, the Chair, and she's booked with someone else that day. And, well, Patricia, you know I'm a professional driver, and I just can't ride with those folks. I've tried, and they scare me to death," she explained. "I'm comfortable with you."

I rearranged my schedule and drove her to the hospital.

In the room before going into surgery, I took her hand and prayed. As I prayed again, I felt something leave her and touch me before departing. As soon as I closed the prayer, Jody's expression had changed into a smile.

"O Patricia, I felt something leave me! And I'm no longer afraid!"

I was always told "fear" is not from the Lord. Yes, fear the Lord, meaning love, respect and trust, be in awe of the Lord and the kind of "fear" she felt will not bother you. 1 John says, "...love drives out fear." (The Bible tells us that God is Love.) Psalm 34:4 "he delivered me from all my fears."

I feel led to share my own experience of this kind. I began to notice a lack of energy and enthusiasm for anything. I had been taught the signs of depression, and my symptoms fit the list. Except, I could not think of a trigger or reason why I might be depressed. I experienced depression when I realized my marriage was not salvageable, but this seemed different.

It was time for my annual checkup. "Dr. Harris," I said, "I've been feeling depressed. It seems to get harder every day to go about my daily activities. I just don't want to do anything. I don't have the energy to do the things I need to do," I confided.

"Patricia, I can't find anything physically wrong. Has anything happened, or is there anything going on in your life that might give you a reason to be down," she asked.

"I've thought about that a lot, and I don't think so," I responded.

"Let me pray for you," she offered.

Several hours later, I was in the Church office printing and folding by hand the Sunday's bulletins. I did not have the energy or will to do this. In anguish, I cried out, "O Lord! Please help me!"

An indescribable sensation started at the tips of my toes and moved up my body and left. As it rose up my body, I felt energy returning! Then the room was much brighter! I felt like 100 pounds had been lifted off of me! And I was filled with energy once again!

"Thank you! Praise you, Lord! Where did 'it' come from?" Immediately, I recalled a strange event about three weeks earlier when I attended a training session required of all Virginia United Methodist Pastors. Clergy from all over the State/Conference were present, including a part-time clergy person from a former appointment who strongly opposed women as clergy persons. Sadly, "the enemy" closes our eyes to the truth of Scripture. Anna was such a prophet who recognized that baby Jesus was the Messiah. In the book of Exodus, Miriam, Moses' sister, is seen leading all of Israel in praise and worship of the Lord. Further, without God leading women, Moses would never have been in place to lead Israel out of Egypt and away from slavery. Deborah, found and described in Judges 4-5, led Israel to victory over the Canaanites. The Judges were persons anointed by God to lead the people spiritually, and as president to lead a nation. My favorite among these experiences is Joel 2:28: "…I will pour out my Spirit on all people. Your sons and daughters will prophecy…."

49

This brings us to The New Testament, which also contains stories of women in powerful roles sharing the faith. Jesus and the twelve disciples had a group of women around them who served in ministry with them. They heard Jesus' teachings. Jesus was pleased to have his cousin Mary choose to sit at his feet with the twelve when he visited her home, while her sister, Martha, chose to work in the kitchen. (Luke 10:38-42) We see the first evangelist, a Samaritan woman, who came to the well and found Jesus there. Their conversation was rich, and she became convinced Jesus was the long-awaited Messiah. She ran back to her village and called everyone out to "come and see" that she had met the Messiah. (John 4:1-42) The villagers came to believe also. In the Book of Acts 1:15*b*, we read that there were one hundred and twenty men and *women* of the Lord's followers (disciples) gathered in the upper room when Holy Spirit came upon them like tongues of fire. *All w*ere anointed. The day Joel spoke of had arrived. God poured out God's Spirit on sons and daughters who went out from there equipped to share the Good News of Jesus Christ.

Such a list makes one wonder why God would not call women to ministry as clergy in this age. God has always used women to fulfill God's purposes.

The clergyperson, who did not believe women should serve the Lord in this way, saw me from way across the large room and immediately worked his way through the crowd as with great urgency and came to me. He greeted me with a big bear hug and then left. I do not think he ever even shook my hand in the past. Two clergywomen friends were standing with me, and they, too, knew him. We looked at each other, puzzled. "Well, that was weird," my friend said. We all agreed. The feelings of depression started soon after. I asked the Lord where "the darkness" came from, and immediately this memory came to mind.

A few meetings after the woman was freed from depression, just as we were about to begin, a couple entered.

"We heard you pray for people here. So, we came hoping for prayer." The woman stated.

She continued, "My husband has liver cancer and is scheduled for surgery in two days. We go in for his pre-op exam in the morning."

"We both believe God can and will heal me." The man said.

Gathered around him, we all laid hands on him and began to pray. I felt the tingling in my right hand again and sensed the urge to put it on the woman's shoulder. I noticed another person near me do the same at about the same moment. They left after the prayer.

Spilling over with excitement and joy, the couple came the following week. The woman said, "The next day, we went to the pre-op exam, and they could find no cancer! The tumor was gone! And I didn't say anything about my shoulder last week. I was putting the surgery off until after my husband was cared for. While you prayed, someone put a very warm hand on my shoulder—and it was healed!"

Healings became a regular event at our weekly prayer time until one night, a member of the church, where we met, came for prayer for the healing of his back, which was scheduled for surgery. He left us in the same condition. We were obviously discouraged. But several days later, he called one of the prayer team members (as we were calling ourselves) and said: "My back was not healed that night because God had greater healing in mind. After my surgery, all four of my children were gathered around my bed, and they began to talk—*for the first time in years*! Years earlier, they fought over something and quit speaking to each other. They would not come to my house if another one were there."

He continued, "As they stood around my bed, they talked for a while and then began apologizing to each other. Soon they were crying and hugging each other."

What a lesson for us! There is no greater healing than the healing and reconciliation of relationships. Often when a relationship is mended, we experience physical healing as well. I believe there is no greater healing than being reconciled to the Lord! And often, we experience physical healing after this reconciliation!

When we surrender our will to God's will, we are reconciled and enter into a wonderful and personal relationship with God. This brings healing to the spirit, mind, and body. Beloved, have you asked the Lord to come into your heart, to be the Lord of your life? Or perhaps you or someone you know is angry with God, or angry and bitter about their life or toward someone, and you or they have several chronic health issues which may well be related to the bitterness and refusal to forgive someone or God. Yes, we must forgive God and, more importantly, ourselves!

Praying and inviting the Lord in is freeing! Scripture tells us that Jesus stands at the door knocking, waiting for us to open the door. Ask, and the Lord will bring about the moment or opening needed. Also, the Lord will provide the words needed to be spoken to free us from the shackles of bitterness and unforgiveness. One of these opportunities occurred when I sensed the Lord telling me to call a man I barely knew (see pp. 87-91). God provides the words that will bring healing. Unforgiveness hurts the one who needs to forgive far more than the unforgiven one is hurt. Unforgiveness is a heavy burden to bear. That is an understatement!

Chapter 12

My Turn

"You do not have because you do not ask God," James 4:2d *NIV*

*"Prayer turns life into a party, into a gift, into a romance…*the more you pray, the more you will experience holy surprises.*"*[18]
Mark Batterson

Although I was participating in a prayer group and team at another church, I continued to serve Bon Air UMC as Chair of the Administrative Board. The youth of our church asked me to lead them on a mission trip to Haiti. I discerned while praying that the Lord wanted me to do this.

I asked the Lord, "But how am I going to be able to help build a school with my shoulder, no both shoulders, in their present condition?"

For several years I heard grinding, almost like sand in the joint of my left shoulder. Now it was more like a chunking sound with much pain. I could no longer reach above the height of my shoulders. The other shoulder was sore and stiff. It was a challenge to comb my hair or close the car door! I knew I had to ask the team to pray for my shoulders.

They gathered around and laid hands on me. After they finished praying for me, there was no noticeable change. I do not recall feeling

---

[18] Batterson, Mark, *Draw the Circle, p. 97.*

any discouragement. I just trusted that somehow, if the Lord wanted me to go on the mission trip, I would be able to do so.

Several days later, I picked some books up to store on the top space over the cabinet. Then I realized—no pain! There was no restriction on the range in which I could move my arms! I experienced no stiffness at all! I whirled my arms in full circles! There was NO PAIN! NO NOISE!

"When did this happen? How could I not notice? Even closing the car door had become a chore, and on this morning, there had been no pain doing that! *And* I DID NOT NOTICE!??" I exclaimed to myself. I was ashamed. Immediately I went to prayer and thanked the Lord for such incredible grace!

Beyond the shoulders being healed, I soon realized as I took the long walk to my car that my hip, which had made a popping or crunching noise since childhood and became sore when I walked the mile or so to and from school, was now free of noise and pain too! *And my knee,* damaged by deep knee bends, no longer gave me pain or trouble when I walked down a long staircase!

Oh, Beloved, if we just believe and ask, the Lord wants to give us far more than we can imagine. Many prayers go unanswered because we never ask. The Lord wants to give us far more than we can imagine. As Matthew 7:7-11 reminds us:

"Ask and it will be given to you; seek and you will find; knock and the door will be opened to you. For everyone who asks receives; he who seeks finds; and to him who knocks, the door will be opened. Which of you, if his son asks for bread, will give him a stone? Or if he asks for a fish, will give him a snake? If you, then though you are evil, know how to give good gifts to your children, how much more will your Father in heaven give good gifts to those who ask him!"

Other scriptures remind us of the importance and power of prayer. Matthew 18:19-20: *"Again I tell you that if two of you on earth agree about anything you ask for, it will be done for you by my Father in heaven. For where two or three come together in my name, there am I with them."*

We hear from St. James 4:2*d*: ***"You do not have, because you do not ask."*** (Emphasis mine. All from the NIV.)

Allow me to offer a few words about prayers that *seem* to go unanswered. Sometimes we pray for God to help someone or to do something that is within our power or abilities. Mark Batterson gives the perfect example. Someone asked him to pray for a computer he could not afford to buy. So, Mark agreed to pray. Mark said he stopped in the middle of the prayer because as he was speaking, he was reminded he had a spare computer he could give the man. So he did!

Sometimes our prayers are answered with a "not yet." When it does not happen in our timeframe, we think the prayer was unanswered or is a "no." And sometimes the answer is a true "no" when it is not within God's will, or it infringes on other persons' free will or well-being. The "not yet" answer can mean it will indeed happen, but it may be in God's time.

I remember reading a true story of a single father who prayed regularly for his three sons to come to know the Lord. His sons tell of remembering seeing their Dad, on a regular basis, on his knees in prayer by his old chair. All three sons are grown and successful in life, but they were not in a relationship with the Lord. At their father's death, they went to his house to divide up his things or to determine what was to be done with them. All three only wanted that chair because they remembered seeing their Dad on his knees at that chair and hearing him pray for them. On that day, they were moved to kneel around the chair and pray. As they did, each gave his will and life to the Lord! It took many years for this faithful father's prayers to be answered. But they were indeed answered!

I prayed and prayed for my marriage to be healed. One night as I prayed, it felt like those prayers never left the space around me. In the silence following the petitions, I sensed the Lord saying "no" because the free will of my spouse was involved. We are not God's puppets. On the "cup is half full" side, I now know we both had a lot of growing to do, and I was freed to go where and to do what the Lord planned for me to do. Until my marriage ended, I was living by my plans, my will. It was a toxic relationship from which we both needed to be freed. Today we are friends, and I love his current wife as my children do.

One of my favorite true stories comes from Russia, the old USSR. There were five sailors on a USSR ship who were Methodists. They met secretly and regularly for prayer. When they were discovered, they were imprisoned for their activity. Seventy-some years later, Russia lifted restrictions to the Christian faith, except that no religion was allowed within its borders that had not been there before this time. When the Methodist Church wanted to send in missionaries and Bibles, the Government blocked admittance until someone found the court record of these five sailors! Since Methodists had practiced their faith seventy-some years before, the Methodist Church was allowed entrance. Think of the faithfulness of those young men, their suffering in prison for their faith, and now they see from the Lord's side what God intended for the salvation and good of others. One can only imagine that this turn of events was the answer to these men's prayers.

Over the years, the Lord healed me many times. There are a few more of those experiences I need to share. One involved a car wreck, not an accident. It was a wreck!

The Mercury Sable began to concern me. The mileage was approaching 100,000, and when I made a right-hand turn, it made a strange noise. As had become my custom, I began to pray, "Lord, please make it clear to me when I should get a new car."

It was June. My niece's wedding was on Saturday at her Mother's Tyler family home, Sherwood Forest, in the Charles City area, where her parents were married. I planned to stay with my son, who now lived in Richmond, Virginia. I had moved to Patrick County, the southwestern panhandle of the State. On the way, I planned to swing by and pick up my Mother in Bridgewater, Virginia and take her to my Sister's home in Mechanicsville, Virginia, so she, too, could attend the wedding.

The traffic on the Interstate was pretty much bumper-to-bumper in both lanes. Traveling at a speed in the 70s miles per hour in the left-hand lane in heavy traffic on I-81 going North, on a curve, I saw in my peripheral vision the car to my right starting to move into my lane.

"She'll see me in a second." I thought. *She kept coming!* In a split-second, thinking, "Do I hit the horn or let her tap me? No, that could cause a huge wreck if we overreact in this traffic and at this speed. I'll keep giving her room." Thinking she would see me any second. However, s*he kept coming over!*

I thought, "Oh no! I had better go into the median!" I prayed, "Lord, please, if anyone has to be hurt or killed, please let it only be me!"

The grass in the median was about knee-deep, concealing the contents beneath. The median changed to just a spit of grass from which a rocky bank rose to 15 feet, obscuring the view of the southbound traffic. The Sable entered the tall grass. As soon as the car went into the grass, the car shook wildly, and the steering wheel was jerked out of my hands.

"Well, you are really in control now, Lord," I thought. "We" (the car, me and some powerful, comforting, shielding presence) slammed into the bank on the corner of the left front bumper.

"Oh! Thank you! No airbag deployment," I thought! It careened around, and somehow on two wheels, I surmised that because of the angle of the car, we then hit on the right side!

"Wow! I thought we were going to roll," I said to the Lord.

At this point, I could feel a real presence over me, with me, protecting me. Perhaps my guardian Angel at the Lord's command? I think so. I felt no fear. I was along for the ride at whatever that might be.

I do not remember how; it was happening so fast, and yet in slow motion, the car was flying up the bank. At the top, the car stopped for a moment as it leaned wildly to the right. I thought it was going to roll over again and down the bank. I calmly said to the Lord, the unseen presence, "Oh no! We're about to roll over! I'll bet you can't get a wild ride like this at any fun park!" And I began to laugh at myself!

I fully expected the car to roll over and over down the bank because of the crazy angle of the horizon. Then I realized that somehow the car had gone back on all four wheels and slid back down the bank toward the highway. Again, the car rolled to the right as if it would go onto its top. Then it slammed back down on all four wheels—again—and spun around and slammed into the bank on the other corner of the front bumper, spun around again. Now *we were skidding sideways into heavy—traffic!* Realizing this, I grabbed the wheel and turned in the direction of the skid, regained control of the car, guided it parallel to the highway, and stopped!

Almost immediately, a man was at my window. "Are you hurt? Boy, are you a lucky Lady! I thought your car would roll over several times," he said.

"I'm okay," I responded.

Two more men joined us. They had pulled over when the wreck started to happen. The first man to reach my car asked, "Are you sure you're okay? Boy, you are the luckiest person alive! I can't believe your car didn't roll!" The other two men agreed.

"There was no luck involved," I said bluntly. "It was the Lord. I could feel Him or someone with me protecting me. I could feel a presence. I wasn't alone!"

The men agreed it was a miracle the car did not roll over on at least two occasions. All insisted it had defied gravity. The first man asked again, "Are you sure you're okay?" The other two men were trying to get the doors open. All were stuck even after I pushed the unlock button, which made the appropriate click sound.

The first man asked yet again, "Are you *sure*…you're okay?"

"Yes, I'm fine, thank you. I felt a real presence protecting me," I responded again. Minutes later, he asked me at least two more times. Doing my best to conceal growing irritation, I asked, "Do you see something I can't see or feel right now?"

"No, ma'am," he responded.

"Well then, why do you keep asking me if I'm okay," I asked and hoped I didn't sound irritated.

"Because I've never seen anyone so calm after such an experience," he exclaimed!

"I told you, the Lord was with me." (Silly, I think that should clearly explain my reaction or lack thereof!) "I had nothing to fear," I said. They finally managed to force my door open far enough so I could squeeze through, and I got out, relieved I didn't have to try to fit through the door window!

As we stood by the road, I wondered if they all thought I was crazy, but I saw this as a great opportunity to witness to God's presence with us. So, I repeated to the little group that gathered, "I just let go and let God be in charge," and said again, "I felt a presence.' A very real presence. A palpable presence surrounded me. I wasn't alone, and I felt no fear. There was a real presence that I talked to through the whole ordeal," I insisted. And I was, and continue to be, eternally grateful that my quick prayer was answered!

A State Trooper arrived in no time. He noted my statement and took the statements of the others gathered there who witnessed what had unfolded. "You are fortunate, lady. These people stopped and corroborated your story. And the person who caused the wreck, well, they never stop and take responsibility. So, I'm sorry, but it'll be on your insurance," the Trooper stated.

Pointing up the road, I responded, "That's not true. The woman who caused it stopped and just now managed to cross the road." All turned to see her coming toward us.

I cannot forget her name. It was the combined names of my sister's first name and my Mother's maiden name, Carolyn Long. I was silently blessing her as she talked to the Trooper and gave us the required contact and insurance information.

"I'm so sorry!!" she gushed. "I just didn't see you until it was too late. I'm on my way to my son's home in Williamsburg to sit with my grandchildren while they go off to the Baptist Church Convention," she said. "He's a preacher."

"You get extra points in my book. No one ever stops when they cause an accident but were not damaged," the Trooper stated.

"O, I could never do that! I'm a Christian," she said.

I felt I already knew that she was a Christian. But the facial expressions in the little group around us spoke volumes. Both of us shared our faith that day—demonstrating how Christ would have us behave. They, too, were a part of this wonderful miracle and answer to prayer. And I am so grateful those men and Carolyn stopped. Maybe without their corroboration of my story, I could be charged with reckless driving.

But that's not the end of the story. The tow truck driver took me to Mom's house in Bridgewater, where there was ample pavement to leave my car behind her house. I called the insurance agent her company referred me to, who just happened to live down the street from Mom. He came shortly after my call.

"It's totaled," I insisted.

He said, "I'm the one who decides if a car is totaled."

"I'm just looking at the obvious," I said with a grin.

"When did this happen?" he asked.

"O, maybe two hours ago or less. And I need a car to go to Richmond for a wedding," I said.

"Well, you've saved us some money by bringing the car to your Mom's. Will she mind if it stays here until we can tow it away? It will probably be the first of next week. And, yes, it's totaled." He continued, "I've got to go back to my office and work on an estimate, but we'll include the money you've saved us. Here's my card, and a number for you to call for a rental is written on the back. They'll bring the car to you shortly."

He called with the estimate...I was amazed. But why should I be? The Lord was taking care of me and providing more. They gave me top dollar for a six-year-old car!

When I finally got to my son Phillip's place, I apologized for being so late; then, I told him everything that happened. "I didn't tell you why I was running late when I called because I know how you worry," I said.

"Mom, I stopped worrying about you a long time ago because I could see how God was taking care of you," Phillip said. "But I think we should go over to Patient First and get you checked out."

The Doctor handed me a prescription saying, just like the Trooper and Insurance Agent had said, "You're going to be pretty sore for the next ten days to two weeks." She added, "Take one of these or take four Advil for the discomfort and swelling." I chose the latter.

Sore! Oh yes! However, I also was healed! Let me explain. I have chronic back problems. Years earlier, the Neurosurgeon predicted I would have upper back trouble. They had "fixed" the lower back problems, but now, the upper back was giving me problems again.

Some years earlier, most of my right hand was numb. I could not hold a pen or anything for a number of days. Bed rest and prayer brought back the feeling and use. My son wanted some batting practice, so we went out to the yard, and I pitched to him. Then there was a hit ball coming toward my face, and I caught it in my glove! Whew! I missed a catastrophe. The next ball was a good hit to my right. I lunged for it, slipped on the grass and went down. I heard numerous cracks! Pain shot up and down my spine. It took my breath away. I lay still, catching my breath and waiting for the pain to worsen. As the seconds ticked by, the pain grew less and less. Odd, I thought as I slowly got up. I had lost some of the rotation of my head, but I could get full rotation—without pain! It just happened (by chance?) I fell just the right way and "cracked my own back," got it lined back in place! There were no more numb hands for years until the month before my car wreck. During the wreck, my back was cracked to the right and then to the left when we slammed into the bank. After the soreness left, it became clear that, once again, my back was healed, and the upper back pain and numbness in my hands were gone! Such healing experiences were answers to prayers.

Remember the first prayer in my story? It was, "Lord, please make it clear to me when I should get a new car." How strangely and wonderfully the prayer was answered, and I had the opportunity to tell others about God's presence during this experience. And along the way, my back was healed, and there was extra money for the car!

The New Car

Again, I prayed about the car, "Lord, lead me to the car you want me to have. I thank you for how you've blessed me with the last two cars." I began to have a vision of a silver, sleek-lined vehicle. I drove to the Roanoke Enterprise Car Sales of the rental cars. After introducing myself, I said, "I need a low-mileage car with four doors." I stated. They showed me what they had available with low mileage.

"Nothing in silver?" I asked. Only a white Chevrolet Lumina fit my criteria. I test-drove it home, noting something about the suspension made me feel carsick going over the mountains. Slightly carsick from the return trip to Roanoke, I arrived mid-morning, knowing I had to find that silver car that kept coming into my head. I returned the car to the dealership.

"There is no way I can use this car. I am always driving over the mountains, and this one makes me carsick," I said to the Salesman. Before I could say more, one of his colleagues came to us and excitedly said, "A sweet car just came in!"

"Is it silver?" I asked eagerly.

"Uh...Yes?" he responded, looking a bit confused.

"Does it have smooth aerodynamic lines? Kind of like a bullet? And low mileage?" I asked.

Still looking befuddled, "Yes, Ma'am."

Now I *was* excited. "That's my car! I've been seeing it in a vision. I want that car!"

"Well, we just got it. It'll need to be detailed before you can see it. It'll be ready tomorrow," he said.

"Don't let anyone else see that car. It's my car! I'll be back in the morning. I only have tomorrow, and I have to turn in the rented car." And I left wondering how crazy they thought I might be.

When I saw the car, it was indeed the car in my vision. It was a 2002 Taurus SES with 14,000 miles on it in the year 2002. Why was it for sale so soon? That's another story I share later of how God takes care of even the little things for us.

A Holy Surprise

When I wrecked the car on I-81, the car defied gravity, and three observers agreed. There was another time, years earlier, when gravity was defied on my behalf. Nestled at the foot of the mountain, almost on but beside of the Rose River in Syria, Virginia, is Mt. Olivet United

Methodist Church. Literally, the building is not much more than two car widths from the River's bank. The early morning Sunday service had ended. The quaint one-room building is set up high, hopefully above flood waters, with a concrete porch and steps across the front. At the bottom of the last step, you put your feet right onto the grass. On this particular day, the grass glistened from an early morning rain. Scattered around the exterior, small groups of worshipers were still conversing. One group was at the top of the stairs, another at the base near the River, and another in the parking area across from where I, as the Pastor, was parked.

As I stepped onto the grass from the last step, my foot slipped out, and I began to fall backward. A split second, I thought, "Can I survive cracking my head on these steps?" At an angle of 45% or more from the ground, the fall suddenly stopped, and before I knew what happened, I was putting my feet back on the ground!

Everyone around the area seemed to freeze. They just stared at me for a moment. No one said a word. Then someone asked, *"How did you do that?!!"*

"I don't know! It wasn't me." I responded, "Something stopped me!" I am certain an angel stopped my fall. Is my Guardian Angel at work again?

At Mt. Olivet Church, God is up close, humble, and personal, and there's a sweet presence in that space. The exterior is white clapboard with three large and long clear antique glass windows with functioning shutters. They are closed after gatherings and faithfully opened by a Trustee just before people gather. The windows brightened the sanctuary and framed the pastoral view of the River, hardwood, evergreen, redbud and dogwood trees and the occasional extra blessings of a buck or great blue herring that grace the area.

Above the altar area hangs a large painting by a local artist of her vision of Jesus. Under it are three plain, sturdy wooden chairs from a more recent era, each boasting a deep red velvet cushion. In front of the chairs was a plain pulpit made of the same dark walnut as the chairs. In front of the pulpit was the altar table that matched the other furnishings. The room boasts no other ornamentation than on the altar table with a gold metal cross and matching candle sticks on either side of the cross. The altar rail is the original, handmade without ornamentation, plain as a farmhouse porch rail, with dark red velvet kneeling pads at the base. The original wide pine planked flooring is dark with age and swept clear and shining. The pews are special as they are the original, antique, hand-hewn straight backs with narrow seats made locally. They are painted white, with the side-arm painted dark brown to match the altar area furnishings. The walls are painted white. The globes, to the large schoolhouse lights, are also white, plain and simple. (Schoolhouse lights hang from a single cord, with a round globe almost flat at the bottom.) The perfect complement to the interior. The high ceiling is more than two stories. To the left of the Altar is an antique organ, still functioning, and on the other side is a piano. The center aisle is covered with a deep red runner that forms a T at the altar. The space is bright, spacious, simple, humble and yet elegant. Upon entering, there is the sense that one can meet a humble and personal God in this place while God's handiwork is clearly on display through the large windows.

The Church facility has no vestibule, no restroom, no phone, no kitchen or classrooms, just one great room. The old potbelly stove that sat in the center of the sanctuary was replaced many years ago with a newer heating and air-conditioning system. Worship in this space offers an aspect of God seldom found in other worship places. The members lovingly kept the building in excellent repair, which spoke of their faithful respect and reverence. In this place, one could find God's peace and humble elegance and majesty as well.

In 1997, I met a Trustee and his wife, the Church Historian, in the parking lot. On the 27th of June, 1995, a flood, declared by experts as a thousand-year flood, had threatened Mt. Olivet, but it survived. Mud, trees and boulders came down from the mountains in the area and caused much destruction, but Mt. Olivet was spared. However, the more recent flood was bigger. Initially, we could not get to the Church to inspect it for damage because of the debris in the roads and parking area. Now in just a little over a year, we experienced a flood that washed out the road from the Parsonage to Syria, and all bridges were out as well—half of one bridge remained.

The Historian laughingly said, "Well, Pastor, now we know God uses beavers too!" She continued, "Thanks to them, our home and the whole village were saved by their dam."

Amused over the prior few weeks, I listened to them as they shared, "Pastor, we've been going by the River just above the Church to watch the beavers building their dam." Then she explained what that dam meant to the whole community and Mt. Olivet. She explained, "When the water and trees came rushing downstream, they hit that dam and piled up, creating a barrier that diverted the river down through the meadow, between the Grave's[19] barn and house and onto the Robinson River! Of course, it prevented all the water, trees, mud and rocks from smashing into our Church, too!"

The Church Historian said, "About 100 years ago, a flood washed the Church building off the foundation and downstream aways, near the end of the parking lot." She motioned in that direction. "Many of the men in the community came with logs. They put the building on the logs and rolled it back to its foundation." She explained further, "Later, they raised the foundation to its current height above the River's bank."

---

[19] Not real name.

We walked around to the back of the building facing upstream and were shocked to see a watermark about halfway up the backside. "That would be about up to or maybe past the Jesus picture!" the Trustee exclaimed.

We walked around to the River side of the building and hesitantly opened the "crawl space" door, a space we could stand in, and we could see it was full of water. So, a bit anxious, we climbed those steps and entered the sanctuary.

Upon entering, the Trustee exclaimed, "O my! The floor feels a bit raised or bubbled up, warped," Trustee said. We looked around carefully. There was no visible water damage.

He then said, "Not a drop inside anywhere! I'll bring a heater down and monitor the floor over the next few days. That should dry out this floor, and all will soon be back to normal."

"Yes, I agree. God used the beavers," I responded.

Prayer with a Vision

Not only does God use beavers or just take care of us, but God cares for cats too! I had recently moved to a new appointment in the Smith Mountain Lake area called Red Valley. Our precious Mendy, a Japanese black bobtail, died from a brain tumor soon after our move. The animal lovers in the congregation sympathized with us over our loss.

The phone rang, and it was Sherri. "I just returned from our Vet's office. There's a sweet yellow cat there that no one has claimed, and they've been trying to find him a home. You may remember several of us at the Church talking about him a few nights ago after the meeting. He loves people and goes right up to visitors. As I was leaving, I heard the Doctor say to staff, 'If that cat's still here when I come back on Monday, I'm putting him down!'"

Sherri continued, "He has a bum front leg. They said someone found him almost dead by the highway, and the Doctor wasn't sure he could save him. Then he lived. But they thought they'd have to amputate his leg, but it mostly healed too. He's so sweet. He's about two years old, the Doctor estimates. I have two dogs and two cats. I've asked around, trying to find him a home. Then on my way home this afternoon, I prayed, 'Lord, I know there is someone who needs that cat. But who?' And you immediately popped into my mind! Won't you go see him, maybe bring him home?"

I replied, "I'll consider it. Thank you for calling."

After hanging up the phone, I called the animal clinic and asked about a time to see the cat when it would fit my schedule. Sunday at 4 P.M., I got the cat carrier out and called my son to go to the clinic. "You're not going to check out the cat, are you?" my son asked as he looked at the carrier.

"Not really," I laughed.

And so "Taco" came home with us. That's the name the staff gave him, but he did not respond to it and Phillip and I found it hard to call him that. It just didn't fit. We kept trying different names. It was frustrating. Maybe for him too!

One morning as I stood at the kitchen door and "Taco" was about 14 feet away sleeping on the hearth, I prayed, "Lord, you know that cat's name. Please give it to me." Immediately I had a vision of a Bengal Tiger! Under my breath, a whisper really, I said, "Ben!" At the hearth, the cat's head popped up; he quickly got up, came to me, sat down in front of me and said, "Meow!" He was twelve years of joy and truly a gift from the Lord!

God cares about animals, and if we ask, God helps us for God's purposes. In my first appointment in Madison, the Lord answered yet another prayer in a wonderful way. It was August, and we had just moved there at the end of June. I had been there long enough to begin to assess the needs of the churches. As I visited with the folks, I found myself praying mightily for discernment and the ability to meet the needs of the people so that we might be the people the Lord called us to be. It quickly became apparent that there was a need for Bible study. I had over forty persons in nursing homes or shut-ins at home, and I was told I should visit this group monthly. The expectation also included visiting every member in the first year! I was new at preparing sermons, and to do this well required a good bit of prayer and time.

In preaching class, we were told that for every minute you preach, you should spend an hour in preparation. Another piece of the stress was that they were largely elderly people, so there were a lot of hospitalizations and deaths. The Pastor is expected to visit in all of these situations. A death adds to the workload a minimum of 15 hours. The average is closer to 20 hours. There was no administrative assistant for the Pastor. The Pastor there was to be the chief cook and bottle washer. Thankfully, my District Superintendent told the churches to cut the parsonage grass or give me an extra day off. It was a three-acre lot with a difficult hill to negotiate.

I share all of this to help you understand my prayer life. I needed help with all these new responsibilities. I was chief cook and bottle washer at home, too, meaning I had to clean the parsonage and handle most household chores, cook, grocery shop, and do my laundry! And so, I asked for help in prayer.

The day I felt most burdened by all my daily tasks, I was sitting on the porch in prayer when my son brought in the mail. There was a letter from our Missionary in Japan. As I read, I began to praise the Lord and cry for joy! My prayer was answered before I even asked! The Reverend Ted Kitchen was about to finish his 41st year of service in Japan, and he was retiring, coming home to Madison. His letter was dated well before I prayed for help.

"Pastor Stover," he wrote, "I will be arriving home on the 15th of August. I look forward to meeting you, and I pray there is something I can do to help you. I have been a professor at the local University here, teaching the Bible. I will be most delighted to help in any way I can."

I felt a huge burden lift. I was not alone. God was meeting my needs at every turn!

Even in Retirement, the Lord Continues to Provide

Retired for a few years, and my car was now thirteen years old. It was yet another car the Lord gave me after much prayer. The odometer was at 140,000 miles. This Toyota Camry XLE gave me 37 miles to the gallon, had a lot of wonderful features, and it rode well, and I never had any problems or expenses beyond the usual maintenance. I was prepared to ride it out until I could not or should not drive anymore. I bought it intending it to be my last car.

Then my daughter gave me a grandchild, and they live about two hours away. It requires travel on I-95 about half of the way. One day she said, "Mom, Griff and I worry about you on the road in that old car. We've been talking and would like to plan a time to come down and go car shopping with you."

It was not long before my son began to mention, "Mom, don't you think it's about time to start thinking about another car? The Toyota is really old."

I replied, "No. My mechanic says she's in great shape and should easily go another 100,000 miles. And I don't want a car payment."

Of the numerous other cars I've owned, I liked it most, some not so much, but they were a practical necessity. I'm embarrassed to say; I *loved this car!* There was nothing wrong with it, and it was the best car I had ever owned; it was paid for, still had good lines and generally looked good! I guess I was attached to it like an old friend or a favorite pair of old shoes that are broken in and so very comfortable. And it was paid for!

As has become my practice, I began to pray, "Lord, you know my children are concerned about me driving an old car. You also know they've offered to take me shopping and help pay for a new car. You led me to this car, and I'm content with it. I feel safe in it. But, if I'm to buy another car, please guide me, make it clear to me you have another car out there for me."

Then my son asked, "Mom if you could get another car, what would you like?"

"Well, I'd like to have another Camry XLE or maybe an Avalon. I'm spoiled now, and it would be hard to step down." I responded while thinking and feeling guilty for my "wants" of an Avalon or Lexus, both being totally impossible for me to afford. By feeling guilty, I mean I believe my money is best spent on helping others.

God is in the business of making the impossible possible. For two years, I prayed about this. I never felt the urge to investigate the possibilities. My children continued to urge me to find a new car. After prayer, I developed a plan.

After my son mentioned this again and I said, "OK. One day I'll go to some dealerships and give my requirements for the next car and ask them to call when they have one that fits the bill. I want low mileage and in a price range that doesn't go over three-hundred dollars a month for payments."

That Saturday, an advertisement on TV mentioned this was Memorial Day weekend, and sales were going on, of course. I felt a nudge, so I asked, "Phillip, do you want to go shopping with me on Monday for a new car? I'll at least leave a salesperson with my criteria."

There we were at the Toyota dealership near our home. Upon arrival, a salesman said,

"Lady, I'm sorry. We don't have any used Toyotas at the moment. It's rare for a low-mileage Toyota to be turned in. Once in a while, we get one because someone is too sick or has died. But again, it's very rare." said the salesman.

"I'd consider a demonstrator, too," I said. "You have my information, and I hope you'll call me if something pops up. Thank you for your time." And I turned to leave, and I overhear…"Mom would really love to have an Avalon." My son said to the salesman.

The salesman said, "Wait a minute. Let's check our other lots around town; we have five, and let's see if something is out there."

In a split second, there was a 2018 Avalon on his computer screen. It was May of 2019.

"What? It just came on the lot this morning! It has 4,000 miles on it. Let's take a look. It's right across the street," he said. "You wait here. I'll go get it."

It was like new. And it was priced at only 2,000 more than I paid for the Camry fifteen years earlier. From the second I saw it on the computer, I had a strong feeling that God had orchestrated this whole thing. The feeling was strong that this was my next car from the Lord. I thought that it was unbelievable. Was the impossible now possible? It seemed so. Why was it here? He didn't know. I knew this car would not be there long. And the sense that God intended for me to have it was stronger. We agreed on the price and down payment!

The next day they called to say my car was ready. As we were finishing the paperwork, the manager came over. "Did anyone tell you the history of this car?"

"No. What is it?" I asked.

"Well, on Saturday, an elderly couple came in and turned it in because they were both having health problems, and they just couldn't afford the payments, and under the circumstances, they really didn't need two vehicles. And she cried. She loved her car." The Manager said.

Please note that Saturday was the day I felt the nudge to go car shopping on Monday, Memorial Day.

The salesman met me outside, and we got in the car for the "tutorial" session. "Let's put your name and address in the computer first," he said. And the computer screen displayed "Mr. and Mrs. Harrison," and under that was "Carol Buchanan." I was a bit stunned.

"O my! Don't erase them yet! My daughter is now a Harrison and a first cousin lives in Midlothian. Her name is Carol Beth Buchanan! Let's check their addresses." I said.

The salesman seemed as surprised as I was. As we looked, I declared, "No, don't erase them! My daughter's in-laws live in Huntingtown, Maryland. I'm not sure that's their address, but it might be!"

Then we turned to the next name and address. "Yes! That's our cousin! That's her address!" All doubt was gone before this that God had sent this car to me, but now...!! God's fingerprints were all over it! And it gave me the opportunity to witness to the salesman!

Chapter 13

The Holy Two-by-Four

"The angel of the Lord came back a second time and touched him and said, "Get up…"

1 Kings 19:7 *NIV*

Have you ever been hit over the head with a two-by-four? More specifically, the proverbial *Holy* two-by-four! I have and I continue to give God permission to hit me again.

When I joined the prayer group, I was in *Disciples Bible Study, Level I.* It was months later, and we had just completed the Study and were sharing in the closing service. As we read a prayer written by John Wesley, a strong sense came to me that this prayer should be read with the Wednesday night healing prayer team. Week after week, I ran out the door to those meetings without that prayer.

One evening I said, "Lord, hit me over the head with a two-by-four to remind me to take that prayer to the group." And I forgot all about it. Weeks later, I stretched across my bed in prayer—deep, wonderful prayers reeled through my mind like a movie. Suddenly, there was the sensation of being touched all over by a gentle yet startling electric shock. At the same instant, the wonderful "HD movie" in my head vanished, and my mind was flooded with brilliant white light and in the light were the words of that prayer!

"OK, God!" I jumped up and arrived at the prayer group with the book in hand, expecting God to reveal the right moment for the prayer's use. That night was different from all the other times. A member of the group, Diane[20], was wrestling with her call to ministry in a new location. When she finished sharing, I offered the prayer with an explanation of the above events. I read John Wesley's prayer from his Covenant Service:

Let me be your servant, under your command.

I will no longer be my own.

I will give up myself to your will in all things.

Lord, make me what you will.

I put myself fully into your hands:

put me to doing, put me to suffering,

let me be employed for you, or laid aside for you,

let me be full, let me be empty,

let me have all things, let me have nothing.

I freely and with a willing heart

Give it all to your pleasure and disposal.[21]

When the prayer was over, she said, "Thank you for that. It is now clear to me what I am to do. I will accept the call to ministry in Florida."

Her confusion was gone, and the burden was lifted. Confidence and the Lord's direction were clear to her as to what path to take. Soon

---

[20] Name changed
[21] *The United Methodist Book of Worship,* The United Methodist Publishing House, 1992, 13th edition, 2011, p. 291.

she and her husband left us to go minister in Florida. They were the second couple to leave our prayer group.

A few months earlier, Sylvia and John[22], God's instruments, had left us. They organized the prayer team and led us to the most wonderful resources, and taught us much about healing prayer ministry. They were mentoring us for our ministry. One evening, they came to our gathering and announced, "Our work here is done. We've put our house on the market, and we will be leaving the Richmond, Virginia, area."

Grief-stricken, we protested. Like sheep, it felt as if our shepherds were abandoning us.

They explained: "For a number of years now, we have been following the Lord's call moving all around the country doing exactly what we have done here. Our work here is finished, and it's time to move on."

We still protested and grieved but knew we had to let them go to wherever God was sending them.

Prayer with Another Vision

One evening, as I prayed for the Church, The Rev. Dr. Franklin Gillis had been with us for a short time; I was startled by a vision: I saw the Bon Air UMC old Sanctuary, now the Chapel of the Church. It was dark. But not too dark to see *it*! In the altar area was a very tall caped, half-human, half-animal creature pacing back and forth. It stopped and looked at me as if it felt my presence in the room! Then it continued pacing. Alarmed, I went to see Pastor the next day. I knew I needed to tell him what the Lord revealed to me. Would he think I'm crazy?

---

[22] Name changed

I said to him, "Pastor, as I prayed yesterday, I saw a tall, dark creature pacing back and forth in the old Sanctuary or Chapel."

Without hesitation, he asked, "What do you think we should do about it?"

"We need to get folks in there and pray," I responded.

Before the week was out, Pastor had organized many teams, consisting of two persons, to go into the Chapel to pray. I was on one of those teams. That was the beginning of improving the atmosphere in the Church building.

PART III:

DREAMS

God Still Communicates Through Dreams

In the following section, you will encounter another one of my experiences with "this present darkness" that Paul speaks about and referenced in earlier Chapters. God created the seen and the unseen. We encounter the "unseen" dark angels and God's faithful angels of light. The wind is unseen, we only see how it affects what we can see: the trees and grass moving, we feel it blowing our hair. Most of us believe there are angels who help and protect us, so why is it so hard to accept that angels, who did not want to obey God, were thrown out of heaven and are also around us, and they too can influence us. They work to take us from God, to bring us to the kingdom of darkness and death.
I believe the number one reason we refuse to accept the reality of "this present darkness" is fear. It is just too scary. If we accept this reality, it might mean we will have to change. That scares us too! But there is power in Jesus' name, in the blood of Jesus and in prayer. Jesus conquered evil when he died on the cross. You may have heard the statement: The War is won. But we have a few more battles to fight. Evil is defeated! Their time is running out!

There are scattered throughout the Bible, signs that God communicates with people through dreams and visions:
Joseph dreams of his family bowing down to him. Later after selling him into slavery and he is freed in Egypt and rises to power, and his family arrives and they do indeed bow down to him.
Joseph, Jesus' earthly father, is told in a dream to marry his betrothed for she was with child from Holy Spirit and to name the child Jesus. Later, in a dream, he is warned they are to flee the country until it is safe.
The three wise men are told to go home by a different route through a dream.
God communicates with Nebuchadnezzar about his future through a dream that Daniel interprets. This is not a complete account of the biblical events where God communicates through dreams.

Chapter 14

The Sheep Will Be Scattered

Soon after Jesus ascended to heaven and the 120 men and women gathered in prayer in the upper room, they were baptized by Holy Spirit and began to boldly preach the good news of salvation through belief in Jesus Christ, the Son of God. This brought persecution from the Jewish authorities and Holy Spirit led Jesus' followers out across the land into other countries. Thousands, Jews and non-Jews, came into a relationship with the Lord and the Church grew. ...Read the Book of Acts.

The prayer team was in its circle reading something aloud together. A deep gravelly voice gradually intermingled with ours and grew louder and louder until he was the only voice I could hear. Then the words on the page turned red! I awoke from the dream alarmed! "This was a warning. But of what? How and why would the Lord allow evil into our prayerful and faithful group?" I wondered.

At the next prayer meeting, the woman across from me suddenly spoke in tongues! This was another first! And immediately Helen, who was to my left, interpreted, "The Lord says, 'Do not fear evil.'"

We took it in, made a mental note of the Biblical foundation, and continued our prayer time. However, we did note that Susan[23], our song leader and guitarist, was not with us again for the third week. She and her husband, Ben[24], had moved to a new location, into an

---

[23] Name changed
[24] Name changed

81

older house, and she was not feeling well. After a few more weeks, Ben, a group member, said, "Susan's dealing with some depression."

"Odd," I thought, "why would she not come for prayer?" She knew the healing the Lord continued to provide to people through our prayer time together. Unfortunately, depression blocks us from moving and doing what can or will bring healing. And, sometimes, prayer warriors are too proud to admit they, too, need prayer. (Not just prayer warriors, many of us find it hard to humble ourselves and admit we have a problem and need help.)

Several days later…

I suddenly became wide awake. The night, like black velvet, was all around, and I sensed a great evil nearby. I prayed, "Lord, show it to me".

Slowly, like a cameo, a partially human and black panther-like face emerged from the darkness. Very slowly, it opened its eyes. They were yellow and glowing cat eyes. I think I shrieked and jumped out of bed and onto my knees. I prayed, "Lord, where is this thing?"

I immediately knew it was in Susan's and Ben's house. I looked at the clock. "Too early to call anyone," I thought, so I prayed and prayed. I saw them in a vision; they were on their knees, hands joined in prayer. Finally, it was seven, and I called. Ben answered. "What's going on over there?" I asked.

He said, "You won't believe it."

"Oh yes, I will!" I responded. Then I shared the vision and revelation from the Lord of the two of them on their knees and assured him I had been praying with gusto for them since being awakened and seeing the "thing."

Then Ben responded, "Both of us were awakened by a noise, and we saw a large black long-tailed creature with a spade at the end of its tail leaving our bedroom! We jumped out of bed, kneeled, joined hands and began to pray. We were still praying when you called."

After a brief discussion about what to do, we agreed to contact the other members of the prayer team to meet at noon in the church where we met weekly.

The Plan

Ben, Susan and I shared the morning's experience, and after prayer, we formulated a plan. Prayer team members would gather at Susan's and Ben's house Saturday morning to "clean" the house.

The proverbial hair stood up on the back of my neck when I stopped in front of the house. I felt an unusual coldness too. "A new experience," I thought. You may have read the expression, "The hair stood up on the back of the neck," but I never knew this was something people could actually *feel*. I admit I did not want to go into that house. Then I remembered the command we were given, "The Lord says, 'Do not fear evil.'" So, as was our custom, we gathered in a circle in the living room and began to pray. Someone let out a soft scream and said, "I felt claws on my back!"

We continued to pray. When the "heaviness" in the room lifted, we moved to another room and repeated the process, leaving several people behind to keep praying. We prayed in the basement next, then up to the second floor. As we started to enter their bedroom, several of us could see a dark cloud filling the room from about waist high up. I thought of Paul's words in Ephesians 6:12: *"For our struggle is not against enemies of blood and flesh, but against the rulers, against the authorities, against the cosmic powers of this present darkness, against the spiritual forces of evil in the heavenly places." (NRSV)*

Entering that "cloud" was not pleasant! Again, we prayed and prayed. Some of the team experienced "depression" momentarily; others identified "murder," "prostitution," and "drug addiction," and there may have been other things I have forgotten. At times, we could feel claws on us. We discerned a strong presence attached to the wall between the bedroom and bath. We prayed and prayed. They were strong, but Jesus is stronger! We prayed scripture, we prayed from the *Prayer Book* of the Episcopal Church and we prayed as Holy Spirit led. Those among us with the gift to pray in tongues prayed in tongues. Something we did not know about each other until that day. Those left downstairs to keep praying called up, "This is amazing! There's a wind in the room and the curtains are flapping and twisting!"

It was winter. No doors or windows were open and this older home had radiator heat. We were seeing the effect of spiritual warfare! The "dark cloud" in the bedroom was almost gone. The house looked brighter and it began to "feel" good. Also, Susan's depression was gone. Tired yet invigorated by the experience, I reluctantly left—the "cleaning" was not finished, but I was expected at home. We all thought this was what the warning, "Fear no evil," was about. And, of course, it was. However, it did not mean just this one encounter.

Chapter 15

It's Time for Change, Again

"The Lord had said to Abram "Leave your country, your people and your father's household and go to the land I will show you."

Genesis 12:1 *NIV*

It was a few years after the "burning bush" experience. The Lord continued to open my eyes and mind, this time through a dream. The sound of someone laughing woke me. And I continued to laugh as I understood the meaning of the dream which would launch me into the next season of my life!

In the dream, I was in the political science class again at Virginia Commonwealth University with Dr. Bob Holsworth when my add-a-bead gold necklace broke and beads scattered everywhere. (I never owned such a necklace.) There I was on my hands and knees, picking up gold beads with classmates helping me. The bell rang for the class to end. Quickly I was left alone to pick up gold beads. I kept finding the precious gold beads, far more than were on the necklace. And they were getting smaller and smaller. I was fascinated! Then I realized I was in the hallway, and there were my hands among the many feet headed to classes while I quickly snatched up beads. And the beads continued to get smaller and smaller.

Then I heard a familiar voice calling me from the end of the hall. It was Dr. Barry Wolf in his white lab coat with several graduate students in their white coats! They wanted to take me to the research lab.

That is when I woke up, and I laughed out loud. I knew immediately what this meant. Though by the world's standards, dropping out of the Master of Fine Arts Program at such a late stage made no sense. However, I was going after something far more precious, more valuable. It was something many people would not understand until they know the value and joy of being in a relationship with the Lord. To me, the gold beads represented God and the ministry to which I was being called.

Chapter 16

The Prayer Team's Diaspora

Israel is scattered across the known world. This is known as the Diaspora in the Old Testament setting the stage for the Gospel to spread across the known world.

The Prayer Team discerned that we would attend a gathering in Exton, Pennsylvania, focused on healing prayer ministry. As we sat in the Hotel eating lunch before the start of the gathering, I began to experience---it is difficult to describe—but it felt like the air, table, floor, and everything around me was shaking, trembling or vibrating. I asked the team, "Do any of you feel anything?"

"No," one after the other responded. "What are you asking?"

No one knew what I meant, so I described this sensation as best I could.

"It's as if everything is vibrating," I responded. "And everywhere we go in this place, there's a sweet smell in the air."

Their eyes got big, and one of them said, "Oh boy are you going to have a great time at this meeting!" I did! I received some inner healing and experienced being "slain in the Spirit", which I have not experienced since. Being "slain in the Spirit" is…I felt like I was floating in a soft white light, like I was enveloped in a cloud as I lay resting on the floor, totally unaware of the surroundings. I knew the Lord was ministering to me, and the peace and rest that time gave me was amazing. I think the Lord gave me a new heart. I was going to need it!

Since that experience, I have learned that some people have the ability to go into a state of ecstasy, which must feel wonderful, but it is not the same as "being slain in the Spirit." I have never been able to do that since. There are those who can fake this experience as well. We attended several more of the healing prayer gatherings and were greatly blessed to sit at the feet of Judith and Francis MacNutt, The Rev. Tommy Tyson (Tommy and Francis both have gone Home), and Don Williams. Don's and Tommy's descriptions of when they were "slain in the Spirit" matched my experience. One of them said, "It was during that time the Lord gave me His heart, and it was the Apostle's anointing."

Not too many people have been able to put into words what they experienced. They say things like, "Rest like I've never had," "Peace, incredible peace," and "Angels were singing," and others have said they knew they were receiving inner and physical healing.

Several of us became prayer team members for these conferences. But I never experienced this blessing again. I did not need to, for the Lord gave me what I needed for the journey ahead.

Back home in Midlothian, Virginia, I was in prayer, and I knew in my spirit I was to call Will[25], a man I met at the Episcopal Church where the prayer team met weekly. I barely knew the man. He was a Psychologist on staff at Virginia Commonwealth University Medical School. Further, I had no idea where he was spiritually or why I was to call or what I was to say! I called my friend, who introduced us and told her about the above prayer results. She gave me his phone number saying, "Call him."

---

[25] Name changed

I dreaded calling almost a complete stranger. What was I to say? I kept procrastinating for several weeks. However, the pressure to call him became almost unbearable, similar to the urging to get up and go to the altar when I was 14.

"Okay, Lord, I'll call him. But please give me the words to say!"

I called. "Will, this is Patricia Stover.[26] We met at Church a while back. My friend Linda gave me your number." I hardly got the words out of my mouth, and I knew exactly what I was to tell him! "This might seem like a strange call," I continued, "but in your profession, I suspect you get a few of those. I was in prayer when I got the distinct impression I was to call you and share something with you."

"Okay, shoot," he said.

"God wants me to share a dream I had years ago: I was with my birth family, Mom and Dad, sister and brother. We were walking on the beach when in the distance, we could see angry black storm clouds gathering and moving rapidly toward us. We began to run to the sand dune walkway that led to our rental house. The storm was fast approaching. I felt great urgency and fear for all of us. So, I insisted that everyone go over the narrow walkway ahead of me. As I was about halfway across, the wind hit me and lifted me. I could see my family with distress and fear on their faces reaching for me and calling me. But I was helpless in the wind. It carried me up and up. I could hardly breathe because the wind was so strong. It was tearing at my hair and skin. I knew I would soon die. So, I prayed, 'Lord, I'm in your hands. Whatever your will.'"

"As soon as I finished those words, I was suddenly embraced in a capsule! I could hear the raging wind all around me, and I could see its effect below, but I floated high above the earth, safe, at peace and

---

[26] Name changed back to maiden name after divorce.

89

feeling loved in the capsule. And I awoke wondering what the dream meant. What was coming our way?"

Still talking to Will, I continued, "Not long after that, I had a vision as I sat in Mom and Dad's kitchen talking with Mom. In a double exposure, I was looking at Mom and also seeing men walk through the kitchen carrying Dad's office furniture and equipment out the back door."

"I believe I was almost in a trance. I remember saying to Mom, 'Dad's not going to need his office anymore.'"

In God's grace, over the years, God has given me dreams and visions of the future that prepared me for change. This was *big!* My Dad was going home to the Lord.[27] I told Will,

"I don't know why the Lord wanted me to share that, but I try to be obedient."

"I know why," he replied. "Without a clue, suddenly my wife announced, almost a month ago now, she was leaving me and our son. I've been so depressed I couldn't work. I am devastated. I just didn't see it coming. I don't understand it. Now you share your dream. I get what God wants me to understand." He continued, "Maybe you can help me with something strange that happened a few days after my wife left. "I was sitting on the front steps of our house. I was really down. I love dogs. Suddenly, there was a beautiful white dog at my gate. It looked like he wanted me to let him in. So, I did. He walked with me to the steps and sat down beside me. I put my arm

---

[27] When I woke from that dream, I could not imagine why after years of no dreams of my parents and siblings, I had this dream. Dad looked 50 at 70. He could still chin himself with his fingertips on the door jam. He was full of life and energy until that summer. "O, it's just a touch of the flu," he said. By November we knew he had cancer and they said maybe two months to live, I had another vision: Neatly typed out on white I saw, "April 25." I knew that was the day my Dad would transition to the next life. It was. And not two months but six months later.

around him and poured out my heart. Then, I began to think how weird this was. I had never seen this beautiful creature before. And I know my neighbor's dogs. As I felt uncomfortable, he seemed to sense it and got up, walked to the gate and looked back as if to say, 'Time to open the gate for me.' He went out and turned right. I leaned out past the hedge to see where he was going, and *he was nowhere to be seen*. Just like that! He vanished!"

"Patricia, what do you think of that? Could it have been an angel?" he asked.

"I believe you know. Yes, Will, I believe it was. He made you feel better, didn't he?" I asked.

"He did." He responded.

"It's my understanding that is one of the purposes for angelic visits," I said.

He thanked me for my call, and I said he would be in my prayers. I never expected to hear from him again.

It was maybe a month later, and I saw him at a Church gathering that most of the prayer team attended. Will was smiling. I could see by his step that he was almost lighthearted as he approached me. "I'm glad you're here. I wanted to tell you what happened that night after you called. I was in bed, almost asleep, when suddenly it felt like my grandfather was behind me as if I were standing up. We were close, and he often hugged me. And just like in my youth, it felt like he had stepped up from behind me and put his strong arms around me. I was fully awake then. I sat up to the side of my bed with my feet on the floor, and I could still feel him there holding me. It lasted for a long time. Like your dream, I felt safe, at peace and loved." He continued, "When it ended, I went back to bed, and the depression was gone, and I slept like a baby!"

To think I resisted the urge to call him and share whatever the Lord gave me to say! Perhaps he suffered several weeks longer because I was not obedient! Both of us were convinced the Lord wanted him to hear about my dream and vision, God caring for me and preparing me, in order to prepare him and open him to his bedtime visitor and healing. And he needed to share about his "special" visitor, the angel who appeared to him as a dog, with someone he could trust or perhaps I fit the category of the stranger on the airplane that people feel safe to pour out their heart. As a result, he knew God was with him and caring for him.

I had to leave that Church gathering early. I did not want to leave. Something strange happened as I drove home. I started singing some of the praise songs we sang at our meetings when I began to hear the prayer team singing loudly and joyfully some of our favorite praise songs, which I just happened to be singing as they sang! And I saw them in the church kitchen cleaning up after the event! It was as if my spirit was hovering there, watching them and singing along! So, I was still with them in spirit! I had this experience one other time a few years later. God is *so good!*

At our next meeting, I shared this experience and told them what they were doing and the names of the songs they sang. They laughed and said they had indeed gotten silly as they cleaned up, turned the chore into fun and were singing those songs loudly. By this time, we had experienced so many miracles that no one seemed surprised or questioned the credibility of my story.

Without realizing it, the prayer team had already begun to experience its own diaspora. Diaspora is the term given to the Jews who went out and were living beyond Israel and were scattered over the known world. The twelve tribes of Israel were scattered. Thus their faith in One True God was introduced to the world beyond their homeland. If there were twelve Jewish men in an area, a synagogue could be established. For example, if there were fewer than twelve

Jewish men, the Jews in the area established a gathering place under a big tree by a river. This provided a way for Christianity to move out to the world as well. The disciples went to the synagogues or Jewish meeting places first to share the good news of Jesus Christ until the Jews began to reject them. Actually, the disciples, Jesus' followers, were sent out by his own instructions and by the urging of Holy Spirit, who was now with them.

Sylvia, John, Diane, and her husband had already been sent out from our wonderful, comfortable little prayer group. The blind woman, Julie, who now could see, had to move to Norfolk, where she found her vocation in counseling. And there was me. It was my turn to leave.

By the closing service of the *Disciples Bible Study* class, I was again feeling pressure to go into full-time service of the Lord--as a Pastor. I was struggling mightily with this Call….

Before the Lord sent me out, there was inner healing to be done. If we are going out for the Lord to teach, lead, and equip others for God's purposes, we need to be as strong and as whole as possible. Everyone has places or pieces of the self in need of healing. And so, it is with me.

The prayer team planned to go to a spiritual training weekend focusing on healing prayer again. The meeting again featured Francis and Judith MacNutt. The teachings, music and worship at these gatherings were always special, and Holy Spirit's presence and power were palpable. Francis was speaking when women around the room began to weep. There were about 700 men and women present, and the Asian women were weeping with hard, loud sobs. It still amazes me…I joined them. Uncontrollable sobs. Francis stopped his teaching and prayed for a few minutes.

"Holy Spirit says not to be alarmed. These women are being healed. They knew before they were even born that they had already disappointed their parents because their parents were hoping for a son. This left a deep wound in their spirit and psychic," Francis explained.

Back home, I visited my college roommate and shared this experience and a new understanding of myself. Leah, "Sissy" to us, said, "I never could understand why you worked so hard to please your parents. As I observed them, there was no explanation for your insecurity regarding them. Now I understand." As do I. This further explains why I felt a need for attention. The day would come when I would hear someone say, "I've never known a more secure person."

At another conference with the MacNutts and the prayer team members, I again received inner healing. It was a time when I was considering a name change. As a child and most of my life, the name "Pat" did not feel like mine. I practically hated my name. In the fifth grade, I recall asking my mother, "Why did you name me 'Pat'? Why didn't you give me a name like Catherine or Margaret or Tish or Tricia, for example?"

Mom smiled, "Your Dad said it was his turn to name you because he always wanted to name a child after his Granddaddy's Civil War buddy who was a redheaded Irishman named 'Pat'. Your Dad said his Granddaddy told wonderful stories about the fellow, and as a boy, he decided someday…someday he'd name a child of his after 'Pat'. Maybe there's a reason you're not comfortable with your name. We agreed on Patricia Jane; Jane is after your great-grandmothers, Frances Jane and Martha Jane. When Frances was dying, she heard the angels sing." She continued, "My family did not like the name 'Pat' because we had a white swayback farm horse named 'Pat'. So, my family started calling you 'Jane'. In fact, everyone was calling you 'Jane' until you were three, and Daddy kept saying to everyone, 'Her name's Pat. Why can't you call her 'Pat'?"

That is the back story to my healing. At the conference, there was much prayer, wonderful music and teaching. Near the end of the conference, the praise band played a new song; I *Will Change Your Name* written by D. J. Butler.[28]

I will change your name, you shall no longer be called

wounded, outcast, lonely or afraid.

I will change your name, your new name shall be

confidence, joyfulness, overcoming one,

faithfulness, friend of God, one who seeks My face.

As we sang, there were invisible arms around me and in my spirit, I knew the Lord was saying to me, "Your parents heard me. I gave you your name; it is 'Patricia[29].'" As we sang this song, I was filled with renewed joy and rejoicing! I always liked "Patricia", just not "Pat." From that moment, I began to try to change my name to "Patricia". (And, I do not understand why, when someone introduces themselves as Jonathan or Patricia, people immediately change it to Jon or Pat!)

Now for the rest of the story! It was years into my journey away from our little prayer team. A new friend, Vivian Utz and I had been getting together every Thursday morning for praise and prayer. She had a diagnosis of fibromyalgia with severe suffering. I laid hands on her many times, and often she experienced healing. One of the conferences with the MacNutts was coming up, and we discerned we were to go. It was held in Stamford, Connecticut. As we were driving, we were listening to our tapes of praise music.

---

[28] Copyright 1987. Mercy Publishing. *Songs for Renewal*, Janet Lindeblad Jenzen with Richard Foster, HarperSanFrancisco, 1995, p. 110.

[29] Several years later, I was in the bowels of the library at Duke University Divinity School doing research for a paper when I stumbled across a footnote: "the name Patricia in its oldest form meant, 'lover of God'."

"Vivian, there's a song from five or so years ago sung at one of these conferences, and while we sang, I received so much inner healing. I yearn to sing it again at one of these conferences. It was, 'I Will Change Your Name,'" I said.

We heard many great teachings from the speakers, Judith, Francis and Don Williams. The final worship was wonderful, and Don was to speak last and close out the conference. The praise band stopped and started to pack up some of their instruments. My heart sank. Then Don Williams literally came bouncing up on the stage, "Wait!! Wait! Holy Spirit says we're not done yet. There's one more song we're supposed to sing…" and he went to the leader and said something. The leader groaned and said, "O, that's an old one."

"OK, everyone, on your feet; we have one more song to sing, *I Will Change Your Name,*" the leader instructed. My eyes are full even now, as I recall the moment. I could not stand I was so overcome. I felt so incredibly loved, loved as if an only child.

Beloved, please know that somehow, God loves each of us as if we are the only one. Each of us is precious in his sight. Jesus told the parable of the one lost sheep, where the shepherd left the ninety-nine to find the one lost sheep (Luke 15:4-7). Our Shepherd is always looking for us, going after the lost and calling like a lover, wooing us to come home to him.

PART IV:

GOD DIRECTS OUR

WAY

Chapter 17

My Call

"The word of the Lord came to me, saying, 'Before I formed you in the womb I knew you, before you were born, I set you apart; I appointed you as a prophet....'"

Jeremiah 1:4-5 *NIV*

One evening not long after the second couple left for Florida, I had to tell the group I, too, was being called away. One Sunday before the *Disciple Bible Study* Class ended, we sang "Here I Am, Lord":

I, the Lord of sea and sky, I have heard my people cry.

All who dwell in dark and sin...my hand will save.

I who made the stars of night, I will make their darkness bright.

Who will bear my light to them? Whom shall I send?

Is it I, Lord? I have heard you calling in the night.

I will go, Lord, if you lead me.

I will hold your people in my heart.

I, the Lord of snow and rain I have borne my people's pain.

I have wept for love of them. They turn a-way.

I will break their hearts of stone, give them hearts for love a-lone.

I will speak my word to them. Whom shall I send?

Is it I, Lord? I have heard you calling in the night.

I will go, Lord, if you lead me.

I will hold your people in my heart.

I, the Lord of wind and flame, I will tend the poor and lame,

I will set a feast for them. My hand will save.

Finest bread I will provide till their hearts be satisfied.

I will give my life to them. Whom shall I send?

Is it I, Lord? I have heard you calling in the night.

I will go Lord, if you lead me. I will hold your people in my heart.[30]

I could not make it through the song. The lump in my throat was too large. I knew the Lord was calling me out to serve in full-time ministry.

When I was a teen, I also felt called, but I did not know women could be ordained as ministers or pastors. I LOVED my work as a research scientist in the biochemistry side of human genetics. I had my own research project, was in charge of three labs, guided, advised, and worked with graduate students, was responsible for some of the oversight of our grants, and maintained a large tissue culture. I worked with a wonderful man, Dr. Barry Wolf, who somehow allowed me to excel beyond what I thought I could do and had me teach graduate students lab techniques.

Although I loved my vocation, there was a restlessness within me that continued to grow stronger. I started feeling awful and had a fever

---

[30] *The United Methodist Hymnal,* The United Methodist Publishing House, Nashville, Tennessee, 1989, p. 593.

much of the time. I recovered over the weekend, only to be sick again by Thursday of each week. Some days I just had to stay home.

When you have allergies, it is wise to become your own detective. I left the last research job because it became apparent I was allergic to guinea pigs—and a feral cat scratch triggered almost every allergic reaction the body is capable of— asthma, hives, blistered corneas, red itchy and swollen eyes, rashes, and granulated eyelids. So, after a few years and finding I was barred from research where there would be animals, I entered research based purely on chemistry. One doctor told me he knew I would move into a pure chemistry research lab and that it was just a matter of time until I would be reacting to some chemicals as well.

As he prophesied, this mysterious illness was due to several chemicals used daily in the lab. I *loved* my work! I did not want to leave research. I was living my dream, yet there was this strange restlessness growing within me which I tried to ignore. I took a leave from my job and found my health returned. I resigned from my job and grieved for two years. Then I started taking classes at Virginia Commonwealth University in areas of interest: political science and creative writing. Professors in both areas encouraged me to enter graduate school. Based on classroom discussions and my papers, the political science professor was convinced I would make an excellent lawyer. With my disability, dyslexia (in my mid-thirties, it was formerly confirmed, then in my forties, I was diagnosed with ADHD), I knew as a slow reader I could never handle Law School or that profession—yet I knew I could if that was where the Lord would want me. However, my spiritual maturity was not yet ready to trust or be obedient to the Lord.

I was accepted and enrolled in the Master of Fine (MFA) Arts Creative Writing program at Virginia Commonwealth University. Several years into the program as a part-time student, and with some success at publishing a few poems, my daughter entered college, my son was hospitalized, and I was trying to work several jobs and maintain the house. I could not handle it all—and the financial burden was huge. Then I had the "gold beads dream," so I dropped out of the MFA program, intending to return in a few years. Then I took the *Disciple Bible Study* class. The internal restlessness returned and grew stronger. The prayer group/team time seemed to increase these stirrings as well. The closing worship service for the Bible Study tied the bow around it when our Associate Pastor, Will White, asked, "Is anyone feeling called into ministry?" I almost spoke but did not. (He later told me he was surprised I did not speak up. He fully expected me to.)

Several nights later, as I prayed, I no longer questioned my call. It was clear that the Lord was calling me to ordained ministry. I began to repeat my litany: "I'm a woman, Lord. I can't speak, I'm a slow reader, I mess up when I read out loud, I'm dyslexic, I'm dumb…," and it was as if an angry voice shouted (I heard no audible voice) "BE STILL!" My brain is never still or quiet. It is always "busy". But for the first time in my life, I *was* still and quiet, with no thoughts running, no distractions. And I sensed the Lord's presence and Holy Spirit working in my spirit. After what seemed like a very long time, I said, "OK, Lord, I don't understand why you would want me, but I'll go where you want me to go if you will always lead and equip me." An amazing peace filled me; the restlessness was gone.

The next day, I contacted Will White, the Associate Pastor and leader of our Bible study class mentioned above. After we met, he sent me to Dr. Gillis, our Senior Pastor. What a long way I have come! From disobedient, rebellious prodigal to one now surrendered. I shared with Dr. Gillis my story of how I was raised in a devoted Christian family, with parents who were tithers and active in many areas of church leadership, and how I fell asleep by Grandmother's light and listened to her loud whisper as she read the Bible. I shared how at the age of fourteen, I felt called, and it stayed with me through my junior year in college, and how I read every book I could find on the world's religions!

With some embarrassment, I shared the well-developed litany that included, "I want to be normal, to marry and raise a family...when suddenly, I felt released to go my own way. I did. Ten years later, like the prodigal son, I was in the far-off country, lonely, empty, and did not know who I was. I yearned to be that child again who talked to God when she played...when I knew the Lord's presence when Jesus was my daily companion!"

I continued to share my story, "In my misery, I began to pray again and joined a home Bible study group and finally found this church home to where I knew God called me." I said to Dr. Gillis, "Now I feel like that child again. I feel like I've come full circle. I know who I am. I am a child of God."

Dr. Gillis asked, "Is there *anything* I can say that would dissuade you?"

I was shocked at the words that came out of my mouth. *"No! Not if this is what the Lord wants me to do!"* I said with fervor and the deepest conviction I had ever felt. And soon after, I was on the way to become an ordained pastor.

And so, I left the prayer team. I stayed in contact with my friend, who introduced me to the group. A year or more later, I learned the group had been completely scattered. They had sensed a call to other churches and other places. One of them was entering seminary. We were like seeds being spread by the wind. Our own diaspora. "The sheep were scattered!"

Becoming a Candidate for Ordained Ministry was made formal after going before a District Committee on Ordained Ministry, where they quizzed me and read the written experience of my Call. They voted for approval. It was now official. This meant I had to tell my friends beyond the prayer team members, my Supervisor at work, Church friends, my children, siblings and Mom. The latter two I dreaded sharing. Those who have known us all of our lives become our personal Nazareth. By this, I mean they know us as others cannot know us, and they keep us neatly set in certain roles or categories in their understanding of us. This includes the cultural norms we grow up with. For example, my mother had not had enough time to adjust to the change in Church practice that now allowed women to be pastors and ordained ministers. I am not sure she knew even one female pastor. Thus, I dreaded her response.

My Church, pastors, children and college friends were very supportive. My decision was fully supported by my daughter, who said, "O, Mom! You'll make a wonderful Pastor!"

"Why do you say that," I asked.

"Because you're a wonderful Mom," she responded.

Then there was Mom. I put it off until I had to tell her why I was moving.

"Mom, I've been trying to tell you something for a while. I'm a Candidate to become a Pastor. I will be going to part-time Seminary and just learned I'll be serving my first appointment in Madison, not far from the family cabin, starting in June." There. I got it out.

She looked stunned. She was quiet for a minute, then said, "I always thought my son would be the preacher in the family." My heart sank. She was thoughtful for a bit longer, then added, "You know, when I was carrying you, I had the strongest sense I was carrying a Jeremiah, so your Dad and I thought you were going to be a boy. I had forgotten about that."

This explained so much to me! I understood why I felt I had to work hard to obtain my parents' approval (as explained in Part III, Chapter 16). This piece of new information immediately excited me because Mother's words seemed to resonate with Jeremiah 1:4: *"The word of the Lord came to me, saying, 'Before I formed you in the womb I knew you, before you were born I set you apart; I appointed you as a prophet...."* It seemed as if, even before I had this information, I somehow knew this. Thus, arose the connection of identifying with Jeremiah when one of the Committees on Ordination asked, "With what Prophet do you most closely identify?"

"Jeremiah and Moses. Jeremiah, because of his call and of his deep love for his people and with Moses because his speech impediment made him reluctant to speak to the people on God's behalf," I responded.

Chapter 18

Temptation Knocks

After Jesus was baptized: "The Holy Spirit led Jesus into the desert, so that the devil could test him." And the devil tempted him three times.

Matthew 4:1-11 *NIV*

In the week that followed the meeting with Dr. Gillis about my Call to ordained ministry, temptation knocked and knocked again. After five years of job applications and a few interviews, I was excited, even expecting to hear I was hired, but I never heard anything. I followed up with calls. They stated that they had decided to hire from within or rehire someone.

The first knock came from one of those interviews. The woman on the phone said, "We did not offer you a position because we believed you were overqualified for the position. We believed you would leave us for another, better position, not to mention we felt you would be bored. Since the interview, we've been searching for a place for you within our company."

She continued, "I'm calling today because we would like you to come in to discuss the details of a new position as director of a new division." The salary was amazing!

"I can't thank you enough." I responded, "I am genuinely honored you remembered me and are making this wonderful offer. But I just committed to another position—I'll be entering Seminary (graduate school again!) and will become a pastor."

The second knock came from a computer software company with whom I had consulted—one of my part-time jobs—and had given the President the best advice I knew how to give after writing a proposition paper for him and some work in preparation for his interview with the loan company. He offered me a job at that time but could not offer me a livable salary. Now he called, saying, "Patricia, I can finally make you a firm offer with the requisite salary. Will you come and be the Company Vice President?" That is *the* Vice President position--in his company!

"Oh, Lord. I should have known all along it was you who closed the doors!" I thought. To his offer, I responded, "I can't thank you enough for your gracious and most generous offer, but I just accepted a position...." Then the third knock came from a growing company that also said they had been looking for a place to fit me in. They were excited to be opening a whole new division and wanted me to be in charge.

"It'll be your baby. You can do with it what you want." The Company President and owner said. Again, I replied as I had to the other two.

What a confirmation of my Call![31] I could only marvel at the work the Lord had done in me. My ambition wanted, or needed, a title as much as a good salary with benefits, yet I felt no pangs of remorse over the response I gave to those amazing offers. I know, also, that God was testing my resolve to be obedient.

---

[31] "Call" is capitalized because we are all called to be in a relationship with the Lord and to serve others in his name. That's with the little "c". Then some of us are called to be set apart for special, fulltime service, the Call.

Also, during the week after saying yes to the Call...

There were several dreams worth sharing. One might fall into the category of a nightmare. Another dream resonates with Matthew 4:1-11 above. After these dreams, I queried several other candidates for ministry about their dream lives after accepting the Call. All reported similar dreams.

In one of my dreams, I was with family and a few friends. It was just an ordinary visit together at my house. I could see a dark shadow nearby and felt like I was being watched. It went where I went. I became uncomfortable and began to run—trying to get away from it. It ran after me. I tried to move faster, but it was gaining on me. I became terrified because I somehow knew if it touched me, I would be poisoned and die. When it got very close to me and reached out a finger to touch me, in that exact instant, I knew it was pure evil, and I cried out to the Lord to help me. And I woke up. I knew I was safe, in the Lord's protection.

Another dream is one of the strangest I can recall. Satan came to me. He took me around the country and tempted me with many things. Then he took me high above the earth and offered me a territory. I kept saying "no" to everything. In anger, he took me to a huge unfinished bridge in the Pacific Ocean and abandoned me there. The bridge was a large steel construction, one lonely section attached to nothing. Wild, angry seas surrounded me. I noticed some human feces on the roadbed nearby. The waves kept getting higher. The spray had soaked me, and it was hard to stand on the now slippery deck. I was alone, cold, wet and very much afraid I was about to fall into the ocean. I cried, "Lord save me!" Finally, I awoke from this horrible dream.

Remember, "Lord help me!" is a big and powerful prayer. Long ago, I learned to ask the Lord to protect me while I sleep and to give me only dreams the Lord wanted me to have, and the Lord has honored that prayer. These dreams appear to be the final tests before entering the ministry of the Lord.

Chapter 19

God Directs Our Way

"Trust in the Lord with all your heart and lean not on our own understanding; in all your ways submit to him, and he will make your paths straight."

Proverbs 3:5-6 *NIV*

In considering my Call, I thought about how God called Abraham away from home and family and led his steps and protected him along the way. God directed Joseph's life for the good of the people called Israel. (Both of these are found in the Book of Genesis.) Even Queen Esther (in the Book of Esther) came to realize that God put her in a place of power so she could save Israel from annihilation. Then I recalled Paul's journeys; Paul wanted to go someplace, and God prevented him from going. There is not one story in the Bible where we cannot see God leading God's people. There are some who have no idea that God is in control of their path! And my path was set by the Lord's Call to Ministry!

As a certified candidate for ministry, I began the struggle to find a way to enter seminary—graduate school again. "Where should I go? What do you want me to do, Lord? The District Committee on Ordained Ministry is urging full-time seminary. Is this the best choice for me?" I prayed.

I was close to completing the Master of Fine Arts degree at VCU. Now I was going to school again on a new vocation track. And my debt was mounting with graduate school loans, and I was responsible for half of my daughter's college expenses. Further, my son would be off to college in a year.

My children asked me one evening, "Mom, why do you keep going to school?"

I laughed. "I just can't decide what I want to be when I grow up."

I had edited a small local paper, written feature articles for it, written and managed a number of grants, audited foster care cases, did research for a law office, consulted for an IT company, found I had some talent for computer programming (learned Fortran and co-wrote a program for our research team), built my own computer, was good at analyzing computer problems—even able to fix them sometimes— and had planned and done training and monitoring of grants in Richmond and Northern Virginia. I was also an administrative assistant who ended up rewriting regulations that a Committee appointed by the Governor was supposed to write. I became the Commonwealth's Immigration Specialist and oversaw a small refugee program in addition to a few other part-time odd jobs.

As I moved toward ordination, I could not see how all of my experiences would be used by the Lord. When I responded to the Lord's Call, I was the Commonwealth's Immigration Specialist managing fifteen million in Federal Grants. It was late January when I began to discern that the Lord was urging me to go into ministry *now*! It became strong. With some hesitation, I contacted the District Superintendent. To my surprise, he said, "I've been sensing the same thing!"

A month later, he called me with a possible appointment. "It will be without any benefits as we can't get you licensed as a local pastor for another year." Then he suggested, "Let's both pray about this for a few days, and we'll talk again."

From the first mention of it, I sensed this was not "it." I called him back and, with much peace, told him, "I have the distinct impression this is not where God is sending me." He agreed. That was the end of it. It puzzled me for several years.

The following year in early February, the urge to go into ministry returned again. The call came. Dr. Chamberlin called once again and said, "I have an appointment for you in June!" Before he would let me respond, he said, "I want you to hear how it came about. The Cabinet had just started to work on appointments. We usually start at the top, dealing with the highest-paid moves and work down the salary scale. For some reason, the Charlottesville District Superintendent brought up an entry-level appointment. As soon as I heard about it," he said, "your name popped into my head. I then asked the Cabinet to put that appointment aside and move on to something else until I could get back from my office. There's something I need to share with you." He continued, "I returned with copies of your paper for everyone where you described your Call to ministry. After they read it, I told them I believe God wants Ms. Stover to go there to the North Madison Charge. It's a Charge of four small, precious churches in the mountains," he continued, "and the Bishop and Cabinet members discerned God is calling you there."

One of the district superintendents later explained to me that there were a number of people just entering the ministry in line for appointments ahead of me, but they all agreed this was a powerful move from God. Yes, this was indeed where God was sending me. I believe someone on the Cabinet told me that I was the first appointment made that year! Extremely unusual and amazing!

In May, I drove to Madison to a "meet your Pastor meeting." I met some of the people, visited each church and lastly, walked through the parsonage. I could not believe it. Well, yes, I could. The Lord still amazes me because in October the year before, I had been to Harrisonburg for Aunt Madge's funeral, and the day after, the whole family with her daughter, Jane Ellen Weaver, wanted to go for a meal at Grave's Mountain Lodge. I had never been there. We were about five miles from our mountain cabin—that's as the crow flies. The road to the Lodge follows the Robinson River. It is beautiful country with well-kept farms with verdant fields of hay and corn, mountains in the background, lovely groves of trees, lazy clear water streams with rainbow trout and crayfish, and views that make a person pull out the camera or an artist want to stop and paint. On the way back down this road, we decided to stop in the revived village of Crigglersville and check out a few gift shops. As I stood on the porch of one of those shops, I took a deep breath of the fresh country air, heard the soft voice of the Robinson River and said to myself, "I could live here," which seemed odd since I thought I had become a true lover of suburbia.

A short distance from the shop, Mom spotted a large brick Cape Cod house on the hill. I glanced back over my shoulder and saw a large sign at the entrance of the driveway that read, "North Madison Charge, United Methodist Church Parsonage." Less than a year later, I was packing to move to that very place! I imagined the Lord had a little chuckle as I made that comment on the porch of the store that day in October.

As I prepared for the visit to the parsonage, I prayed, "Lord, I don't deserve anything." And I remember asking, "If possible, could you please keep me near the mountains or near water? But I submit to go where you want me to go, and Lord, thank you for sending me to the mountains. And Lord, if possible, could the parsonage please have a nice porch and some daylilies like Grandmother had—I have such good memories of those flowers?"

That evening as I turned the car around to leave the parsonage, I saw not just a small bed of daylilies as I imagined, but the backup lights lit up a long row of daylilies in front of the wall at the top of the cliff that bordered the driveway. Then as I was driving out of the driveway, I looked back over my shoulder for a departing glance and saw a porch on the side of the house! How good the Lord is! My next two appointments were in the mountains, the second in the mountains of Patrick County (literally, we lived on a mountain), and the third was in a valley and very near a large lake, Smith Mountain Lake in Franklin County—mountains all around. (I write this chapter in an office with a view of a harbor in the middle of the Chesapeake Bay on Tangier Island.) Again, how good the Lord is! How incredibly my prayer was answered!

The prayer for daylilies continued to be answered at the next stop on the incredible journey on which the Lord sent me to the North Patrick Charge, serving two precious churches on the middle tier of mountains in Patrick County, Virginia. There was a bed of those wonderful orange daylilies in the backyard next to the storage shed. I overheard several women complaining about the deer eating all of their flowers, especially the daylilies. "That's odd," I said, "my daylilies haven't been touched, and there are two to five deer around the Parsonage every day."

This was a puzzle until one day, as I ate lunch and looked out back, I saw something strange happen. A doe and fawn were eating their way toward the lily bed. The doe soon reached out to bite a lily blossom and quickly jerked her head away as if stung or smacked on her snout. She tried again and the same reaction. The fawn reached for a lower bloom and behaved exactly like its mother. And the pair moved on into the thicket where the blackberries were ripe. "There must be a bee problem out there," I thought.

After lunch, I walked to the lily bed and looked all around the area. Not one bee was to be seen. In seven summers there, I never lost one bloom to any plants around the house or that flower bed either!

To some, we would just shrug our shoulders and move on. But I know the Lord was continuing to answer my prayer for daylilies and daily prayers to protect me and my home. Perhaps there was an angel

113

stationed there by the lilies who smacked the noses of the fawn and doe? It's the only logical answer! (Written with a grin.)

Back to the Madison Parsonage…

I was settled into the beautiful parsonage in Madison when one day, in conversation with a parishioner, who had come to the Parsonage Office, somehow, the subject came up of how my appointment there came about.

I was saying, "I know from this experience that God does indeed make our appointments, as some people question God's hand in the appointment process. It does not mean we humans are always obedient, but God does indeed direct our appointments. Humans do not always get it right away. However, God will intervene, when necessary, until those in the appointment-making process get it right."

Then the woman shared, "Last year around January, the former Pastor told our Committee she was going to ask the District Superintendent for a new appointment, and then maybe a month later, changed her mind!"

"O my! Last year in January, my District Superintendent and I discerned that God was calling me to enter the ministry then. But a month later, that 'sense' was mysteriously gone! It puzzled both of us. We were confident I was being called out at that time. Thank you! Now I understand what was happening," I said.

My assertion that God was without doubt in charge of our appointments was confirmed! So clearly, the Lord planned for me to be there.

My next appointment was God's appointment, too,…they all were!

The Dreams and the Next Appointment

For many years, since childhood, dreams of new places and faces came to me—later, they happened; I mean, they really came to be. First, there would be a Deja vu experience, and then the dream would be remembered. Like when we moved to Harrisonburg, and I knew my way around the school and recognized faces I had not seen before—except in dreams, of course. I believe now this was God's way of keeping me open to the gifts of Holy Spirit, and it protected me from adjustment to new places. Even when I went overseas, there was never any culture shock—because, in a way, I felt I had already been there!

Then, the dreams began again with people and places I had never seen before. I should know by now that the Lord is preparing me to be called to a new place. My son shared that he, too, was having "those" dreams again. I had settled in and was looking forward to a sixth year with the churches in Madison County, Virginia. But those dreams troubled me. The flesh is weak—I did not want to move, not yet. It was exciting to see what was happening there among the people. My love for the people was deep. Further, I was nervous because I realized I had put down roots and become comfortable. Note that word "comfortable." In that condition, I often lose my edge, my being in step with God's will and sensitivity to God's movement among and through us. I begin to rely more on myself than on God. I move away from the Lord because I become more self-reliant, feeling that "I" am in charge. That is not where I want to be, and it is not where a true servant of the Lord can be. As disciples, we lean in on the Lord. In that state, the Lord can equip and use us, and God receives the glory. Vividly, I recall the day I realized this—and said, "Uh-oh. You're going to move me, aren't you, Lord?"

I was reappointed for a sixth year; I had a great confirmation class underway, as well as a level *III Disciple's Bible Study*. The churches were growing in faith, outreach and attendance. But "those dreams continued."

It was the eleventh hour, literally. About ten after eleven P.M. on Saturday night, my District Superintendent called. He said, "I have a great appointment for you! There are two churches in Patrick County that don't have a Pastor. The current Pastor is an ordained elder, and you will be getting a good raise. They've never had a woman Pastor before, but their DS thinks they are ready for one since the churches are very matriarchal."

He continued, "Let me know your decision on the morning of the last day of the Annual Conference. These two churches in North Patrick County have met with three different pastors, but their DS just knew (through discernment) these were not the right persons for these churches. At the late and last-minute Cabinet meeting tonight (Conference was starting the next day), the Bishop asked for all of the DSs to make suggestions for this appointment and said, 'I don't care if it's not an ordained person—These churches need a pastor!'"

My DS continued, "When I heard the church's profile, I knew you were the perfect fit. Several other DSs said your name came to mind as well. So, it was agreed to ask you to move—if you're willing."

After I hung up, I called a friend I knew I could trust with confidentiality and asked her to pray about this with me. After very little sleep and restlessness, I arose, troubled, unsure. My friend called early Sunday morning and said, "Patricia, you will know by noon what the Lord wants you to do."

The early service was going great! I was getting excited. I just knew the Lord was telling me to say "no." However, our musician did not show up for the service. A young man, the son of a member, was visiting and had filled in as our musician before.

"Neal[32], will you please play for us this morning? It looks like Leah (our pianist) isn't coming."

He quickly looked at the bulletin and said, "I don't know that last song."

"Well, just choose a substitute and announce it when we reach that point," I said.

He nodded in agreement.

Again, I was starting to feel almost giddy because I knew I would not be moving, that is until he stood and announced, "Turn in the brown hymnal to number 142, 'I Will Go Where You Want Me to Go.'"

"O no!" I thought. And we began to sing…

It may not be on the mountain's height, Or over the stormy sea;

It may not be at the battle's front My Lord will have need of me;

But if by a still, small voice He calls To paths I do not know,

I'll answer, dear Lord, with my hand in Thine, I'll go where you want me to go.

I'll go where you want me to go, dear Lord, O'er mountain, or plain, or sea;

---

[32] Name changed.

I'll say what you want me to say, dear Lord, I'll be what you want me to be.[33]

Holy Spirit fell on me in great power. I struggled through three verses! I could barely stand, and it was all I could do to fight back tears. I went for the car without seeing anyone to drive to the next service. In the privacy of my car, I "lost it." Sobs racked my body. It felt like my heart was breaking. I loved these people and this place sooo much. I prayed, "Lord, I have to lead and preach another service. I can't do it like this! You've got to help me!"

With the Lord's help, I got myself together, led and preached again and went home, packed the car and drove off to the Virginia Annual Conference with two delegates from our churches. I ached to tell them, but I could not do so before reporting to the two district superintendents.

Over the next two days, one minute, I was saying "no," and sometime later, I was saying, "Yes, I will be obedient."

On the designated morning, I entered the civic center early. There stood three DSs (all friends for a number of years, one was Dr. Gillis), and as they saw me, I noticed their faces fell. They were obviously excited about the new appointment. I walked up to them and said, "I'll go."

They burst into laughter.

Puzzled, I asked, "Why are you laughing?"

"Your body language was telling us—no way will you go!" They responded.

---

[33] *The Cokesbury Worship Hymnal,* C.A. Bowen, General Editor, The Methodist Publishing House, 1922.

"The spirit is willing, but the flesh is not," I responded. That was the truth!

On August 15th, six weeks after we United Methodists usually move, I moved to Patrick County to serve two more precious churches. I felt like my heart had been torn out of my chest. I prayed and prayed for healing of this grief and to enable me to love these people as much as those in North Madison. Leaving them was like leaving a baby I had birthed. There was a part of me that rejoiced because it was clear again that the Lord had made this appointment. I knew the Lord sent me to this place I knew absolutely nothing about, but it was in the mountains—and I had daylilies! Yet my grief was heavy. "Please, Lord, don't let this pain shut me down or close them out," I pleaded.

It was the second Sunday of this new appointment. Before my arrival, the Church leadership called the congregation to pray for the church and new pastor each Sunday before worship. They never had a woman pastor, and some were threatening to leave. So, the Lay Leader called them to prayer. I joined them again on the second Sunday. As we gathered in the large Sunday school room, I looked around the table as the prayer began, and suddenly I knew what was going to be said next, and then I remembered the dream. It was one of "those dreams" that had troubled me because I did not want to move. I remembered each face and each word spoken—and love for them swept over me. I recalled that during the dream, I said to myself with surprise, "These people are praying for me!" And more of those dreams came to be. God is so good!

The next dream, I should say dreams, of note, may seem a bit more fantastic for anyone to believe. But my son can verify that this is true. In fact, God has given him this gift as well. I took the week off to write my ordination papers. It was a good week. I had more time for focused prayer, and I enjoy writing—I always have. It was Monday.

The writing was going well. I was really focused and crunching out the pages when the double-exposed film began...or vision began.

Rolling before my eyes was dry, barren and rocky land rolling by as if looking out of a moving vehicle. I scolded myself for allowing my mind to wander. It stopped—for a short time, then it was there again. The remainder of the afternoon, I fought this as I tried to concentrate and continue to write.

Tuesday started off great, that is until the vision of rocks and tan dirt started rolling before my eyes again. Again, I fussed at myself for not focusing. Suddenly, I saw a few buildings like I had seen in pictures of the Holy Land. I stopped typing and asked, "Is that you, Lord? Are you telling me to go to the Holy Land?" I laughed and said, "Well, you know you'll have to provide the resources!" The visions stopped, and I forgot about it.

Two days later, my dear friend, Vivian Utz, called. She laughingly said, "Patricia, we're going to the Holy Land! I've raised enough money for three of us to go. I know you. You'll have to pray about it for a few days and call me back."

"No, I don't need to pray about it. The Lord has already told me to go." I responded. And I shared the "pesky" visions. This was at the beginning of Fall.

In March, the dreams started. It seemed I had dreamed the entire night. I remember waking myself with audible groans and sometimes as I started to cry. After a number of nights like this, my son asked one day, "Mom, what are you dreaming about? I keep hearing you groan, talk or even cry."

"I'm dreaming I'm in the Holy Land. But I can't remember any more than that." This went on for maybe a month or longer. My son expressed fear for my safety. Vivian wanted him to go with us, but he refused. He did not want me to go to the Holy Land because of his fear. I assured him, "Since it's clear the Lord told me to go, I will be safe."

Shortly after entering Israel, I began to remember my dreams. I had, as I said earlier, been there before. One day we visited a Palestinian professor who kept a watchful eye on the building and expansion of Israel into Palestinian territory. The room was dark, so we could see the slides of graphs and satellite photos. When he began to speak and the first several slides came up, I remember thinking, "I have heard this presentation before. I already know all of this. I've seen these graphs and photos. How is this possible?" Confusion reigned within me for a moment. Then I remembered. I *had* dreamed it—all of it in its detail. I was so glad the lights were off! The tears were streaming down my cheeks, and I struggled not to sob so others would not hear me. I put my sunglasses on just before the lights came on so my companions would not see I had been crying. I kept asking, "Why God? Why did you reveal all of this to me? What is the purpose? How am I to use it?"

I do know that I did not experience any culture shock. Was this one of the reasons why? Another thing I remember vividly: I felt like I had come home. How strange. I loved the people, and I was in great pain with the oppressed, with Israel and the Palestinians and their struggle. I did cry, moan and groan. The emotions were exhausting.

I found peace by the Sea of Galilee in the town of Tiberius. When the trip was over, I realized I previously dreamed much of it!

It was a while until I had those types of dreams again. We were still in North Patrick after seven blessed years, and my son Phillip and I began to have "those" dreams—seeing faces we did not know and places we had never seen before. We agreed that God must be preparing us for another move. He was!

Along the way, from time to time, I was tempted to drop out of the path to ordination. It was time-consuming and emotionally draining, and stressful, as the studies, class time involved, volumes of reading and paper writing that competed with the ministry time needed to serve the churches and community. Plus, there were responsibilities to various District Committees and activities, and I served at the Conference level as well, which meant a day of travel: four hours to Richmond and four hours back. Many denominations have pastors who serve churches without completing their education and the process or steps required to become an ordained person. I often prayed about whether to continue in the required steps to ordination or to drop out. However, I continued to discern that the Lord had a purpose for me to become an ordained elder, a member in full connection with the Virginia Conference. A number of elders continued to encourage me to stay on track with Word and Sacrament ordination. (Meaning to preach and administer the Sacraments of Holy Communion or Eucharist and Baptism.) This did help. However, this meant more time away from the flock as we met for special training events, spiritual growth training, lots of writing papers, going before committees to be examined for our knowledge and anxiously waiting to find out if we passed or not. I often thought that we should have Ph. Ds after completing the process. Something we all knew but did not talk about was that ordination moves one into a higher income bracket. My two rural churches could not afford a salary increase. Many members were factory workers. Then the factories closed because their jobs went to Mexico and overseas, and our churches struggled to meet our financial responsibilities. For five years, there were no raises for the Church staff--me. If I became a fully ordained person, I would have to move. Before this became apparent, Phillip and I both began to have those dreams again.

Those dreams became a reality in the first several meetings and gatherings at the new Church, but normally these dreams were rather mundane. However, another one of those dreams came to me after about a year or two at the next location, in a valley surrounded by mountains in the Smith Mountain Lake area. This Parsonage, too, had lots of daylilies. I was now ordained an elder and, for the first time, serving one church with more than a staff of one. In addition to myself, we had a Church Secretary, Youth Director, Music Director and Sexton! All except me were part-time paid positions.

I remember waking early and sitting on the side of the bed for a moment as I remembered clearly the dream that just awakened me. This in itself was unusual. Usually, I cannot remember any details of these dreams after I wake. "Why would I, Phillip, and his close friend Daniel be in a graveyard measuring off a plot?" I asked myself aloud.

Several weeks later, I got the call. "Pastor, will you please come to the house? Dad just passed from an apparent heart attack." Daniel said.

As is the custom, we offer to help people in such situations in any way we can. The next day Daniel called again. He asked, "Pastor, will you and Phillip meet me at the graveyard on the hill just past the Burnt Chimney Church around one P.M.? I need help measuring off the family plot. The Cemetery Trustees aren't available to do it."

A few hours later, there the three of us were in a graveyard measuring, and I remembered the dream. We were close to this family, and as in the past, this prepared me for this sad experience.

God Directs Our Paths

Years earlier, I read a story in the *Guideposts Magazine* that my parents always had around the house. The story seemed to be stuck in my head more than others. A young couple and their infant child lived in an urban area. On this particular day, the infant would not stop crying. He was hungry. They were out of milk, and there was no money to buy more. They prayed that God would somehow provide milk.

A man was on his way home, and as he sat at the stoplight near the young couple's home, he got a strong urge to take a detour to the grocery store to buy milk and take it to the house on his right. He did just that!

I can still imagine the joy all of the people in the story felt. I yearned to be that kind of follower of Jesus, to be so in tune with the Lord that I could trust such an urge and act upon it. Fortunately, over the years, this happened often.

For example:

It was getting dark. It would take forty-five minutes to get to the meeting in Charlottesville. I was really early in leaving, maybe twenty-five minutes to spare. As I drove down the road toward Madison (the town), a strong urge to stop by "Aunt Elizabeth's" came to me. (I heard the Utz family refer to Elizabeth so often. In this way, it became my frame of reference as well!) When I came to the road to Aylor, Virginia, I turned right toward their farm past Oak Grove United Methodist Church. The field on the left was full of grazing deer. The drive is pastoral and peaceful to the soul.

At my arrival, Aunt Elizabeth excitedly called to me to hurry inside. Her husband was on the floor in obvious distress. Quickly I called 911 and called Vivian, who lived a short distance from the old farmhouse. Only moments before I knocked on the door, he had started to show signs of trouble. Vivian was a rescue squad member and nurse and was there before you could blink and began working on her uncle. I took Elizabeth aside, prayed with her and did what I could to calm her. She asked me, "Pastor Patricia! How is it you arrived just as this was happening?"

"I was on the way to a meeting in Charlottesville when I got a strong urge to go to your house. The Lord sent me."

Another time I recall clearly is worth noting. Some Sundays following worship at Mt. Olivet UMC, a precious one-room Church on the bank of the river, someone would hesitantly say, "Pastor, I wish you would go visit 'Bill'. He doesn't know the Lord and really needs to."

Bill's wife often attended our services. Yet, the Lord had not led me to visit her home. What I mean by that is, on the days designated for visitation, I got up and said, "OK, Lord, who do you want me to visit today?"

I would get a sense that I should turn left or right from the driveway. On this particular day, after several years of different folks at Mt. Olivet asking me to visit Bill, I got the urge that today was the day to visit him. I knew from their hesitation and body language that there was some reason why they were concerned about me visiting this man. I could never have guessed why!

On this cool and beautiful sunny spring day, I turned right and drove toward Syria, Virginia and the little hollow where Bill's family lived. I could see his truck and her car in the driveway. The house was small and neat, cuddled in a half-moon of trees with redbud blooming in abundance. In the country, nearly thirty years ago now, the older folks were uncertain about making appointments with the Pastor for visits. The downside of this was that sometimes those we hoped to visit were not home. Yet, they preferred surprise visits, unlike the younger members who preferred a phone call and appointment. Fortunately, they were home.

I was warmly welcomed into the home. Briefly, we made polite small talk. I looked around at the family photos, noting the blessing of their grandchildren. Almost abruptly, Bill's wife jumped right to the point.

"Pastor, I don't know what brought you here this morning, but you couldn't have come at a better time. A short time ago, we got a call from Bill's Doctor about his test results." Her voice cracked a little. Bill looked like a deer blinded by a spotlight. She continued, "Bill has cancer all through him. They said he doesn't have long to live."

I replied, "I can tell you the Lord sent me here today. I've had you on the list to be visited for maybe two years. On the days I schedule for visiting, I always ask the Lord whom to visit today. This morning there was a clear urge to come here."

We talked a little more, and we prayed. Bill willingly took my hand as we prayed. "Would you like me to come back soon?" I asked.

"Yes, as often as you are led," they responded.

I visited them at least once a week. I always asked the Lord for the words to pray. I think it was on the third visit or so we stood together and held hands, "Lord, we are sinners gathered here in need of your great love, presence and forgiveness. Heal us spiritually and physically. Grant us faith that there is healing for us here and now and in the future. Lord, we humbly ask you to come into our hearts, forgiven and renewed. We accept you, Jesus, as our Lord and Savior. Thank you for loving us and accepting us as we are. We pray in your precious name, Jesus, amen."

When I looked up, Bill had big tears streaming down his cheeks, and I could see a new light, even hope, in his eyes. I knew in my spirit that this had been a tough and independent man who now stood before me, broken and renewed.

For eight weeks, I visited until his death. What a celebration we had at his service of resurrection! After the service, family and community gathered for a meal. A small group of Church members gathered around me.

"Pastor, you have to know that we were all scared to ask you to visit Bill. You see, many pastors have gone to visit him over the years, and he ran every one of them off at the wrong end of a gun. We were shocked the first time we saw your car parked in his driveway, and then we saw it parked there numerous times after that. We were excited and just couldn't believe it." One of them said, "I asked Bill what was different about this Preacher. And he responded, 'She didn't come here thumping her Bible and with a holier-than-thou attitude.'"

I was blessed to be able to tell these sweet people that Bill accepted Jesus as his Lord and Savior in those weeks before his departure and transition into new life.

PART V:

GOD IS ALWAYS

PRESENT

"Jesus said, 'Remember, I am with you always, to the end of the age.'"

Mathew 28:20*b NIV*

Chapter 20

God Continues to Direct Our Path

"So do not fear, for I am with you; do not be dismayed, for I am your God...."

Isaiah 41:10 *NIV*

It was my third year in the Smith Mountain Lake area of Franklin County, Virginia. The Youth Group was active, there was much community outreach and mission activity, plus two members were starting the process as Candidates for Ministry. It was March 4th. Every year, beginning in February, United Methodist Pastors expect a call to inform them of the Cabinet meeting for appointing pastors. Some will be appointed to stay at their current appointment while others move to new appointments.

My District Superintendent called. As expected, he said, "Patricia, I'm happy to inform you that you are reappointed for another year to Red Valley." That was good news. So, the genesis of plans already in my head for the summer, fall and winter could begin to be fleshed out.

My Mother was in her 90's, so attending her birthday gatherings were never missed. It was the 14th of March on our way to celebrate when my cell phone rang, and it was my DS again. Puzzled why he might be calling, I heard the excitement in his voice.

"Patricia! I have a wonderful appointment for you!" I had heard from colleagues that if elders (the ordained ministers with full connection to the Conference) are told, "You have an appointment," you could not say "no" if you wish to continue serving a church. My DS continued, "It's the perfect fit for you. It's a close-knit community that you like. They love Bible study, have a number of active prayer groups, have a large active youth group and are very mission-oriented. You're more of an evangelistic preacher, and they love that!" He continued, "We're sending you to Tangier Island!"

Stunned. I had never been there! I was familiar with the Chesapeake Bay because my husband and I owned a cottage on the Bay and spent many weekends and vacations there. I heard good things about Tangier from my parents' visit there in the 1960s, and my husband enjoyed a week there duck hunting in the 1970s. He raved about the food from Hilda Crockett's restaurant. Tangier is a small island in the middle of the Chesapeake Bay. It is only accessible by ferry from Crisfield, Maryland, which runs year around. During the summer months, two more ferries run, not always daily, from Reedville and Onancock, Virginia. There were only two cars and three pickup trucks on the Island. Folks walk and ride bikes and golf carts to get around the Island.

In my last appointment in the Lake area, we were three miles from the Roanoke County line and six miles from the city of Roanoke. At the time, there were four hospitals in Roanoke, and the Medical School from Virginia Tech University had a large presence there. Yet, Phillip and I had difficulty finding doctors willing to take on new patients. Interestingly, this was the point of contention that family members used to object to our moving to Tangier Island. Family and friends urged me to refuse this move. I knew these were expressions of care, love and concern for Phillip and me. Yet I felt quite harassed. The harassment came in other forms as well.

It was 2009. Later, I would assess this year as one I could not classify! Phillip's medicine was working so well that he was able to attend college classes again and, he was doing well when at the snap of a finger, it stopped working, failed, and he was hospitalized. I do not recall how many hospitalizations followed. In time, I became very sick because of exhaustion. More than a month later, I finally shook the chest and ear infection. Well, not totally one ear; it lasted for four years.

While all of this was going on, the appointment to Tangier came! This was not an offer. I had no choice but to move if I wanted to continue to serve as a Pastor. I was running back and forth to the hospital to visit Phillip while trying to keep up with my ministry. On one occasion, I hit a deer in my fairly new Camry Toyota. On the way home from the body shop, I stopped at the Post Office in Boones Mill, and someone backed into my car, wrecked it again and drove away! Also, I learned that the body shop missed a big dent made by the deer in the hood.

While doing all of this, I was packing for the move to Tangier and handling a long list of detailed things one has to do when moving. In the meantime, the HD television, only seven months old, died, and I spent hours and hours on the phone trying to get the warranty to repair or replace it. What a huge time consumer! And it added to the stress—harassment.

Upon arrival at our parsonage in Tangier, I learned there were big problems with the Parsonage. I did not think we could live there and remain healthy. It was dark and moldy, and I questioned the safety of living in the structure. I noticed the second floor sagged. This involved many, *many* conversations with the new DS and then the Church Trustees. They planned to go in and paint some the day before we moved in...until they went in for the inspection after the former Pastor moved out.

It was Friday before our move on Monday to Tangier. I had just picked up my car and driven to Danville, Virginia, to pick up Phillip from the hospital. The staff at the hospital was reluctant to release him and were considering moving him to Norfolk, so he would be closer to where I was moving! It meant an hour on a boat to Crisfield, Maryland, then maybe another two to three-hour drive to the Norfolk hospital! On the first of the week, I managed to convince the staff to discharge him on Friday.

Most of the packing was finished. Then on Friday evening, I got a call from Tangier. It was the Church Secretary charged with calling me about the Church Board's decision, "Hello, Patricia. The Board had an emergency meeting last night and decided we could not move you into the Parsonage. We fanned out and looked at a number of houses to move you into. We are moving you into a rented cottage until we can repair the Parsonage. It's small, Patricia, so you need to label your boxes for storage or to go with you to the cottage." It was much too late for that, I wanted to say but did not.

At this point, I was exhausted, listening to family and friends telling me not to move there, dealing with packing, the TV, hospital staff, car, closing my ministry and closing the parsonage, while making preparations for the next Pastor; *and* I had difficulty finding a mover! I finally found a company that would take us to Reedville, where our stuff would be placed on a barge and transported to the Island.

It was Monday after the Friday call and the morning of the move. The movers were loading the truck the supervisor concluded was too small, so another one was scheduled to come later. The Church Secretary from Tangier called again, "Patricia, the Board canceled your barge this morning. They need you to meet the boat at the dock in Crisfield, Maryland, and they will move you over. The things you need to store will be stored in the Church's storage shed near the dock where we have kept the Church van," she said. "Oh! And one more thing, one of the nurses on the Island made an appointment for your son to get his blood test at the hospital in Crisfield." Then she gave me the directions to the hospital and indicated we needed to be there at eight the next morning!

This was one more detail on the long list providing more stress! Fortunately, the mover was almost finished loading the first truck, and the second one arrived, but I had to go to the supervisor and tell him of the new development, "I just got off the phone with the folks on Tangier. They canceled the barge your company hired and said we have to meet their boat at the dock in Crisfield, Maryland. I don't know what this means for you," I continued, "However, it means we will have to spend the night somewhere close to Crisfield, so we can be at the hospital on time for my son's blood test and then catch the mail boat over to the Island at noon."

He looked as shocked and disgusted or discouraged as I was! It meant an unplanned night on the road for him and his crew. The movers knew it would take the better part of Monday to load. The original plan was that the truck/s would go to their warehouse for the night while the crew went back to their homes, and early the next morning, they would drive to Reedville to load the barge. This now meant they would drive as far as they could toward the boat rendezvous point after they finished loading, find a place to spend the night and then get up early and drive to the dock in Maryland. The movers took this in stride, at least in my presence.

My dear friends, Vivian Utz and Wenda Singer, took time off from their jobs to come and oversee the rest of the packing (Vivian seemed pleasantly surprised I had done so much packing, she helped on previous moves), and her sense of humor lightened the stress. Vivian borrowed her son's pickup truck and loaded it with house plants, and followed us to Maryland, while Wenda returned to the Richmond area with the promise of coming to the Island in a few weeks to help us unpack.

133

On the long drive to Maryland from Franklin County, Phillip and I had the two cats, sweet Ben and Chester, who was about 19 years old, black and white with peacock blue eyes, and Ben, who was three, an orange tabby or ginger as the Brits call them. Chester cried the entire way while Ben slept peacefully.

We made it to the hospital in time for the blood test, which was required to refill his prescriptions (just a little more stress). We also needed to find a doctor as soon as possible since he had been discharged from the hospital several days before.

Later at the dock. The boat was too small. The Captain and crew had a short list of what the Church Committee said they should bring. Vivian met the boat ahead of us.

"May I see your list, please," she asked.

"We're only to bring what's on the list, and the rest is to go into storage over here," one of the men said.

While looking at the list, Vivian said, "Oh, I see. So, they don't get to take any of their clothes except what they have in the overnight bags? What about her office supplies, books, and pots and pans," she asked?

Captain Jerry replied, "Well, I don't know anything about that. This is what they told me."

"Well, here's what we're going to do," Vivian said. "We're going to put as much stuff on your boat as possible while Patricia and family catch another boat over."

"Patricia," she continued, "you sit right here as stuff is loaded off the truck; you tell them which box stays for storage and which ones go on the boat."

I did the best I could, but the crew mostly ignored my instructions and put boxes and furniture where they wanted. It was all very disorganized! Many of the things we needed, like summer clothes and shoes, were nowhere to be found on the Island: no pots and pans. The cottage was sparsely furnished. Phillip slept on his mattress on the floor. It was much like camping out. I could not do much cooking because of the limitations of the cookware. I finally found my winter coat in storage in Crisfield in late November. We did not find many of our clothes for two years. In the meantime, we bought new shoes and clothes. We had things stored in two places on the Island and the rest in storage in Maryland across the Bay.

I have moved a number of times in my life, with my parents and as an adult before and after becoming a Pastor. Without question, this was the most challenging, most difficult, most frustrating---I cannot think of another adjective—except to be blunt once again—it was the move from hell! We survived, and so did the Church. It was hard on them, too, and they continued to struggle with compassion and perseverance on the parsonage issue.

Then there was some good news. The Church already had three corporate prayer times a week. They were hungry for the Word and really knew the Bible, and there were about fifteen gifted, really gifted lay preachers. There were 25 to 30 youths in the Wednesday night youth group. The attendance at the two Sunday worship services was great, and my leadership was accepted. They were warm, caring and loving in welcoming us. Some folks told my son they thought I could really preach. It was not easy preparing two messages each Sunday because a lot of the same folks attended both services. The Wednesday night service required another message. They were accustomed to the lecture style of Bible teaching/study, so I had my work cut out for me!

The Church had a gifted praise band. Before we arrived, the Band prayed for a bass player. My son is a gifted drummer. One night at practice, they told him, "Phillip, you're the answer to prayer. When you told us you were a drummer, our drummer said, 'Let him have the drums. Where's that bass? I've always wanted to learn to play the bass.'" The former drummer was quickly picking up on playing the bass guitar. The Islanders are so musically gifted and creative.

My family on both sides gave me a hard time about this move—that added unneeded stress. However, it served to convince me that the Lord had great things in store for us on the Island. As the move became more and more difficult, I felt Satan was making it as difficult as possible to convince me not to go. I assured family and friends that the Lord had always provided for Phillip's and my needs, and I would continue to trust the Lord would provide.

My biggest concern was finding doctors for Phillip. In the last location, we could not find a personal care provider, and as for the doctors who provided his treatment, I did not have a lot of confidence in them. But on the Island? The Lord does provide! I shared our medical needs with a few people, and the nurse knew he had just been discharged from the hospital. They gave me the telephone number of a couple of doctors who flew in every weekend to the Island. They helped at the Island clinic. On occasion, he flew an Islander off to the hospital. They were Doctors Susan and Neil Kaye from Delaware. I made a phone call, "Dr. Kaye, this is Patricia, the new Pastor on the Island. Nurse Jean told me to call you. She arranged for my son's blood tests, but we need a doctor to approve it and refill his prescriptions. Also, he was just released from the hospital, and someone should see him soon."

Dr. Kaye asked, "Can you two be at our house at 2 p.m. this afternoon?"

Excited, I responded, "Yes! We'll see you then."

"Please, call me Neil," Doctor Kaye said. "So, Phillip, you have five different medications, I see. If we can get the dosage of this one up to a clinical level, we can eliminate three of these. Would you like that," he asked.

"Yes," Phillip responded. "Definitely."

Then Dr. Neil explained, "I did some of the first clinical trials in the US on this drug. It's the best one for your symptoms. So, we'll increase it."

As I sat listening and mulling over this news, I wondered if the Lord went through all this trouble to get Phillip to the doctor he needed. Our God is an extravagant God. I do not doubt this was a great move from the Lord. (Interestingly, I would not have been eligible for this appointment if I had not been ordained an elder. It was a long process that I often considered dropping out of, but I always discerned the Lord wanted me to continue.)

The doctors and Physician's Assistant, Inez Pruitt, who lives on the Island, took us both in immediately. And the following summer, the clinic located a short walk from the cottage moved to its newly constructed facility—directly beside the rental cottage!

On the shore, we had to go pick up our prescriptions. On the Island, they are delivered to your door if they come in on the mail boat. In fact, we were quite spoiled. Almost anything and everything was delivered to our door. Dr. Neil refused to let us pay him. He did not want insurance. He was seeing a number of Islanders, and they were all doing quite well.

There was also plenty of seafood. Phillip once caught a 25-inch rockfish (or striped bass when found in freshwater) in the creek behind the cottage. The Island had a beautiful beach, underused, which we did not get to enjoy as often as I would have liked.

We went to the well[34] every other day to fill jugs with drinking water—no need for Brita anymore and some exercise to boot! We walked to the Post Office, Church, grocery store, ice cream parlor (only two doors away!), shops and restaurants. I could walk to visit about half of the Church members.

And God Continues to Guide Our Path, Even in Retirement

Two years before mandatory retirement, I began to pray for the Lord to prepare a place for us, hopefully in the Richmond area where Phillip's Dad and family live, plus my Mom, my siblings and a nephew and many friends still live there. Hopefully, we could pick back up with at least some of our doctors in that area.

As suggested by the DS, I called the Manager of the Clergy Housing Corporation. It was October 2014.

"Hello, Bob. This is Patricia Stover. I will be retiring at Annual Conference next June, and I am hoping to find housing in the Richmond area."

"Patricia, there's nothing available in that area. There's a condo in Roanoke that is in a 55 and older development with a low HOA fee. It's fairly new. And a house in Winchester might open up." He responded,

"I really need the Richmond area because my 99-year-old Mom is there, as is Phillip's Dad and his family, aunts and uncles, and cousins on both sides of the family. I've been praying about this for two years. Is there anything? Any possibilities?" I pressed.

---

[34] This reminded me of Rebekah at the well, Isaac's wife, and the Samaritan woman at the well where she met Jesus.

Bob responded, "Well, we have a one-story townhouse that might open up before June, but it's in the Mechanicsville area."

"My sister and nephew live in that area! I know that's to be our place!" I said excitedly! "Can you hold that for us?"

"How old is your son? That will take the Board's approval. Plus, it's in a 55 and older community with a higher HOA fee than the one in Roanoke. This one has an indoor pool, a small gym and is a very active community."

"Please do what you can," I said after sharing Phillip's age.

Several weeks later, Bob called me back. "Patricia, it's Bob. The Board approved your request, and the house will be available by the end of January. We will clean and paint it in March. You can move in any time after that."

I responded, "That's wonderful news. I've found a mover, and we scheduled a moving date of May 9th." Then Bob agreed on a time for us to visit the place. During our visit to the house, I discovered that my sister lives five miles (as the crow flies), and my nephew and family are literally five blocks away in the single housing portion of the development. In addition, there were numerous doctor's offices within two miles of our place, and the local hospital is only two miles away!

So, I continue to rejoice in the provision of the Lord for our needs. There was the question of, "Why the Hanover County area." But I just accepted it as God's incredible grace. There is no question about that. However, once again, we had trouble finding a doctor to care for Phillip. The private doctors and PAs could not fit him in when problems arose with his medicine once again. We learned he was eligible for care through the Hanover Community Services Board (CSB). We also learned that it is the best one in central Virginia and one of the best in the State. His Doctor with the CSB is very much another Doctor Neil! She's awesome!

It's almost like God likes to show off! The Lord does indeed take delight in providing for us if we just ask. Then God gets the glory! And I praise the Lord for providing what we could not do for ourselves.

Chapter 21

God is Present Indeed!

"Come and see...!"

John 4:29*a*

God is Present Indeed!

God is Present Indeed!

"Hello!" I said into the phone.

"Hey! I'm OK!" said the voice on the phone. It sounded like my brother Ed. But confusion reigned.

"Huh? What do you mean?" I asked.

"I survived the tornado!" the voice responded. It was my brother!

"What are you talking about?" I asked. A huge tornado hit the Petersburg, Virginia, area the afternoon before. The News reported four deaths in the Walmart and some destruction in the old town area. I was selfishly glad I did not know anyone in the area. However, I did pray for those affected by the storm and planned to donate extra to help families.

Ed responded, "I was with a mission team working on a house in the old town area of Petersburg when the tornado hit. We didn't have much warning, but we lay on the floor in the safest room we could find. While it was over us, I had to peek. Above my head were a lot of wood splinters swirling like a bunch of toothpicks."

"When it was over, we were all relieved to be OK. Most everything outside had changed and was barely recognizable. All our supplies were gone except for one bucket with a few tools in it, and it was still sitting in its place in the front yard, undisturbed. So strange."

He continued, "The people across the street were just emerging from a cinderblock room and the only thing left of their building and business. We joined them."

"Someone asked where the fellow from Oklahoma was. They all looked around and noted that his truck was nowhere to be seen. They said he pulled into their lot, jumped out of the truck and ran to them yelling, 'Quick! Follow me! There's a tornado about to hit!' They all followed as he led them to the office, the cinderblock room inside the metal building. He told them to lay down on the floor and not to look up until it was over."

"Now he was nowhere! One of the crew said.' The Owner asked the Manager, 'Did you order something from that Company?' The Manager responded, 'I've never ordered from them. I thought you must have.' The Owner said he never had either. 'Then how…? And how did he know we had this office inside?' We all concluded it had to be an angel!"

"Ed, that's amazing!! I think you're right! It was in the news last night that people in the Walmart reported complete strangers, who were not employees, grabbed their hands and rushed them to the back of the store where there were cinderblock walls just minutes before the tornado hit the store! They concluded there would've been a much higher casualty number. The people interviewed said that the people who led them to safety were not with the group in the 'safe place' during and after the storm. They said they concluded these persons were angels."

Some of you who read this may not have been old enough or were not even born when we experienced the September 11th, 2001 tragedy when the two towers were struck by airplanes in New York City. There were a number of reports of someone's hand taking theirs in the blackness of the buildings after the planes hit and a voice telling them to just follow. When they got to where there was light, the person disappeared! After hearing a number of reports like this, they concluded, and I agree, angels were busy that day too. The official reports stated there was an unusually small number of people in the towers that morning. Normally, they stated, there would be as many as 50,000 people in the buildings. Person after person shared stories of how they were delayed that morning or they would have been there in their office. I doubt if any of the official reports will include such stories. They cannot be proven as divine intervention. However, they cannot be disproven either. With the eyes of faith, we know and understand.

So beloved, when you have moments of inconvenient delays, relax and do not stress. God is in control and may be moving to protect you. I believe God protected me from losing my car one day.

I found a free parking space on the street near the Main Street Train Station in Richmond, Virginia. This was one of the part-time jobs, and parking fees would take a big bite out of my paycheck. The location was convenient to the Monroe Building office tower where I worked.

On this particular morning, Phillip missed the school bus. That meant a long drive to drop him at school and then go in the other direction to work. I was exasperated and embarrassed at how late this would make me. Of course, my parking space was taken, and I had to drive around, taking more time, to find another space and then a long walk to the building. It turned out to be the day a train derailed and crashed down on the cars parked in my space. I do not believe in luck.

Bad things happen to good people all of the time.[35] I hope the railroad's insurance compensated those who lost their cars that day, and hopefully, it was enough to get an even better replacement than they had before. The Bible reminds us that the sun shines on, and it rains on the good and the bad. The difference is that when we are children of God, we do not go through it alone, and sometimes a seemingly bad event can provide a blessing in disguise. Sometimes, we learn to become stronger and better after going through a rough spot. Our faith can be strengthened if we put our hand in the Lord's hand and trust. Jesus taught us to trust God like little children must trust their parents. Through the eyes of faith, there is always hope, and we will see a "silver lining." God sees the whole picture when we can only see a small part. That day I decided never again would I stress over a detour or something delaying me, always reminding myself it just might be keeping me from something awful.

Speaking of something awful reminds me of the promised answer to the question asked in Chapter 12: "Why in 2002 was I able to buy a low mileage car, Taurus SES 2002 model, from Enterprise Sales?" This is the rest of the story! God really does care about us and the small things.

The car was great until the weather got warm. Like all cars, it got hot in the sun. The parsonage did not have a garage or carport, and most places I went to were in the sun as well. The heat brought out a pungent odor as if something had died in the car. I found Downey Dryer sheets under the seats when I bought the car. Guess that was a warning of what was to come! I tried to identify the location of the problem and sprayed carpet in the cabin and trunk, but nothing helped.

A colleague clergywoman and I started the required Pastoral Chaplaincy training through Wake Forest University's hospital program in Winston-Salem, North Carolina, winter-spring session for

---

[35] This is a big subject which I can only touch on here. Harold S. Kushner, wrote *When Bad Things Happen to Good People,* a good discussion of this topic.

two days and one night each week. Once the warm days set in, we had to deal with the smell as I drove my car from my house to the school/hospital.

One day she asked to take my car to the grocery store during her time off duty. I had to serve as Chaplain during that time. When I got to our room, she was frustrated and apologizing profusely. A large plastic liquid laundry detergent container fell on its side and cracked open, spilling much of its contents in the trunk. We scrubbed and wiped for a long time. Even after we returned home, there was more to wipe up. However, the good news was that the smell was gone forever!

Through the eyes of faith, I see this as one of God's little serendipities. Just a coincidence? I see the Lord's fingerprints in such events as these, one of God's little miracles. I have had countless such bottles in the trunk to fall over, yet never a problem with one of them. It just happened when we needed it that my colleague bought the rare jug of detergent with a weak spot! What are the odds of that? God's little miracle.

God Really is Present and Cares About Us

In the spring of 2001, I sensed we were being called to prayer—it was strong. I shared with the two churches and the County-wide ministerial group. (In some areas, the pastors form a group to come together and share in ministry and provide moral support for each other. Generally, it is county wide and ecumenical—all Christian clergy persons.) I pleaded with folks to join me in prayer. Once or twice one or two showed up. When the pastors made the commitment to come on a set date, oddly—not really oddly (because the enemy will do most anything to keep us from prayer—that's where we have power over him), one had strep throat, another had pneumonia, another overslept. No one came. I prayed—I wasn't feeling 100% myself. Month after month, I continued to ask them to come to prayer.

Finally, with a tone of urgency and with some disgust, I said, "I'll be at Woolwine UMC on Tuesday, September 11th, at 7 am. Please join me. I sense it's urgent—we *must* pray!"

I was there praying when one lay woman came in. I had moved to my office but was still praying. She joined me there. As we prayed, suddenly, I was struck with a crushing burden of grief that I could hardly bear! I collapsed in deep sobbing. I could hardly talk. My companion was alarmed and about to pick up the phone to call 911.

"It's not of me," I assured her between sobs. "Something awful has happened, I mean *awful,* and the Lord is grieved, and many will be grieving." I don't know how long I wept. Then the phone rang, and since I was in no condition to answer it, my companion answered. It was a fellow pastor, Kaye, who said, "I intended to join you there in prayer, but the TV caught my attention as I walked through the family room. Do you know what's going on?"

My companion responded, "No. We've been together since about 7:30 A.M. in prayer."

Then Kaye shared, "The twin towers have been hit by two airplanes. And the second tower to be hit just collapsed."

My companion asked, "What time was it when the tower was hit?" When she heard the time, she was amazed. She said, "Not long ago, Pastor Patricia collapsed in whales of grief and said to me, 'Something awful has happened, and many will grieve.' I looked at the clock almost immediately and saw it was 8:45 A.M., the exact time the tower was struck!"

In the next several weeks, two other friends, one a part-time pastor, said, "I was on the way to work when I felt a heavy burden and call to prayer. Now that I think about it, I'm amazed at the content of my prayer, and I know it was Holy Spirit-led. I was praying, too, when the tower fell, but I did not know it at the time I pulled off the road because I was so overcome with grief I couldn't drive, and I whaled for some time before I turned the radio on and heard the news."

Another woman friend said, "I was in my shop next to the United Methodist Church in town and felt compelled to go into the Church to pray. As I prayed, suddenly I collapsed to the floor and cried and grieved as I've never felt before." She continued, "I also learned a short time later that it was at the same time the tower was struck."

I've wondered what would have happened if we had been obedient and prayed as I sensed the Lord calling us to pray. I know it was Satan who blocked our prayer times. I remember I didn't feel very well one morning when I went off by myself to prayer. I was fine after I prayed, and no one ever joined me that day.

Beloved, Satan will do all he can to stop us from being the people God calls us to be. He will do all he can to keep us from praying—he knows this is where our power and strength are—this is how we can be part of God's miracles, God's work. Look through the Gospels. See how often Jesus prayed.

A favorite scripture is Peter's miraculous escape from prison in Acts Chapter 12. After killing Jesus' disciple James, which seemed to please the Jews, King Herod put Peter in prison. Four squads of four soldiers each were guarding him. Meanwhile, the church is gathered and praying for Peter. The night before Peter was to be tried, he was sleeping between two soldiers, bound and chained, with two other soldiers as sentries at the entrance. Suddenly, an angel appeared. He struck Peter and woke him. "Quick! Get up!" the angel said, and the chains fell off of Peter. He was ordered to dress and then to follow the angel. Peter thought he was dreaming. They passed the guards, the iron gates opened before them, and after a long walk, the angel left him.

Then Peter realized this was no dream or vision. So, he went to the house where the church was gathered and praying for him. I love this next part: Peter knocked at the door, and a servant girl answered the door. She recognized Peter and was so overjoyed that she left him standing there and ran back to the others and exclaimed, "Peter is at the door!" (v. 14) When they heard this, "You're out of your mind." She kept insisting it was true. "It must be his angel," they said.

So, they were there for several days praying for Peter's protection and release, their prayers were answered, but they did not believe it! Oh, how human we are. Meanwhile, Peter is still knocking at the door! When they saw him, they were astonished! (v. 16) Then Peter shared how wonderfully their prayers were answered.

Another time I witnessed God's presence and care was during my first pastorate and the flood in Madison County. We lived on the road that runs by the Robinson River. Fortunately, the Parsonage was on a hill across from the river. I heard stories of one hundred years before, the river bed was behind the Parsonage, but it changed course during that flood. A lot of the town folks took refuge on our hill. The Parsonage was built soon after WWII in the late 1940s, which means it wasn't there at the time of that flood.

We had rain for a month (as best I can recall) almost daily. It was three to five inches each time. The rivers were staying high, and the ground was saturated. I remember looking out of the beautiful antique glass windows of Mt. Olivet Church in Syria and noticed the water was almost to the base of the church building. We had another three to five inches of rain that day.

Several days later, on June 27, 1997, the deluge came. Vivian, who was a volunteer with the rescue squad, said, "I started calling everyone to put them on alert. The station was notified by the National Weather folks that the radar was showing black over us. And they'd never seen it go black. They urged us to get folks out of the low-lying areas and away from places where the mountains might come down. They estimated it might dump 20 or more inches in an hour…AND the storm was stalled over us!"

It was trash pickup day. Two of our area women owned the business and were already making the rounds. Judy[36] told me, "Our next turn was down the Robinson River Road. But there was an officer at the intersection blocking the Road. To our surprise, when we got there, he motioned us onto the Robinson River Road. The Road was already flooded. We didn't get too far, and we were stuck. We either ran off the road, or the flood had already washed a section of the road out. So, there we sat."

Meanwhile, further up the Road, two of my neighbors who lived across from the river on flat land were told to evacuate. Ruth[37] was in her early seventies, and her mother-in-law was in her nineties. Ruth said, "Mom didn't feel up to going, so we decided to stay. It's been a hundred years since it flooded. We'll be all right. Then I looked out front, and the water seemed to be rising pretty fast. So, I hurried Mom out to my truck and started down the road toward Town.   We didn't get too far past the Parsonage when the truck started to float and was being swept downstream. Suddenly we stopped moving when I heard a bump. Water was filling up the cab pretty fast. Someone banged on the back window. It was Judy! We were now wedged up against her garbage truck. She had jumped into the truck bed and wanted us to climb through the window and get in the truck with them. When I looked back into the cab, Mom was curled in the fetal position and wouldn't move. Somehow, we finally convinced her to join us. Of course, with our help."

After the flood was over, Judy finished her story. "The Officer who directed us to turn down the road wanted to know how we got there! I told him, 'It was because you directed us to turn there!' He

---

[36] Name changed.
[37] Ditto.

said he never let one vehicle go down that road, and he had no recall of seeing us. He insisted he never let us or anyone go down this road!"

The Coast Guard had already been called in. They rescued the four women by helicopter and two kids who were clinging to a spindly tree next to the Parsonage after riding their bikes over to see the flood and getting caught in it.

How would you explain the garbage truck being in the right place at the right time? Beloved, God is present in our lives. We just do not always see it, except maybe in hindsight.

Powerful Times of God's Presence and Care

Is anyone of you sick? He should call the elders of the church to pray over him and anoint him with oil in the name of the Lord. And the prayer offered in faith will make the sick person well; the Lord will raise him up. –James 5:14-15a *NIV*

God cares about us. It was my first year at Duke Divinity School. Students are not allowed to miss classes "unless you are in the hospital," is how they put it. I had some brief conversations with my next-door neighbor about being involved in healing prayer and seeing amazing healing.

"Hey, Patricia! Brenda[38], who lives on the next floor, is packing and has called her husband to come to take her home. She has a fever and is in a lot of pain from an earache. I told her roommate about your experiences in healing prayer, and she asked me to bring you up to pray." My neighbor Mika[39] said.

---

[38] Name changed.
[39] Ditto.

"O wow! You mentioned you had a little experience with this, right?" I asked.

"Yes, a little," Mika replied.

"Well, good. Because it's better with two or more," I said and reached in my purse for the vial of oil given to me by the MacNutts at the last Conference.

Brenda was feverish and flushed. Her roommate introduced us, "Brenda, this is Patricia. She's experienced in healing prayer, and I asked her to come and pray for you. It's such a shame that you have to leave when we're almost halfway through the summer session. Will you let her pray for you?"

"Well...I guess so." She said hesitantly. I could see skepticism.

Then I said, "I need you to sit down and get comfortable. Will it be okay if we lay our hands on you and I anoint you with this oil? I might put my hand over your ear. Which one is it?" I asked. She pointed to one ear. And so, I prayed out loud and then without voicing my prayer. In about ten minutes, she said, "The pain is not as intense."

"I noticed, too, that you feel a little cooler," I said. She agreed. "I think you will be OK. You might want to call your husband and cancel his trip here." I suggested.

She looked baffled, amazed. "I'll leave now. I think you're going to be fine."

Then I returned to my room. About forty minutes later, Brenda burst into my room with her roommate behind her, "Patricia! What did you do!? My fever's gone, and a few minutes ago, my ear opened up, and the pain is gone! How...what??"

"I didn't do anything! God did it. Brenda, you know, in the Book of Acts, the Church, which is the people, they were constantly praying for the sick and bringing healing. And in the Book of James, we are instructed to do this. I believe God is here and is still in the healing business if we just believe in Jesus' presence and power. It's really that simple. And as a young person, I yearned to see the Church *be* the Church we see in the Bible. I still yearn to see it!" I confessed.

"My husband is a biochemist, and he just doesn't believe this!" Brenda said.

I replied, "That's interesting. I was a research biochemist. The Lord has been working on me for years to get me back to where I knew His presence and just trusted and believed. I don't think these miracles break the scientific 'laws' necessarily, but that the Lord just speeds up the natural process. But I also believe God can do whatever God chooses."

The short version of the story is that Brenda finished that year, and she wrote me the following Christmas that she and her husband were leading healing prayer in their congregation.

The following year at Duke Divinity School, we planned a healing service in the Chapel. One of our classmates had a bad limp. Some of us took turns walking with him from the dorm to class. When the time came for the invitation for people to come forward for anointing and prayer, he went forward. A group of us gathered around him, laid hands on him and prayed. The Bible came alive before our eyes. All of a sudden, he was jumping, running up and down the aisle and shouting praises to the Lord!

In the Book of Acts, Chapter 3, verses 1-8: Peter and John went to the Temple at the time of prayer. A man who had been crippled from birth was brought to the gate where he would beg from those who were entering the Temple courts. Of course, when he saw Peter and John, he asked them for money. Peter and John looked at him, and then Peter said, "Look at us!" When they had his full attention, they told him they didn't have any silver or gold, "But what I have, I give you. In the name of Jesus Christ of Nazareth, walk." Peter took his hand and helped him up. Immediately his legs straightened and were made strong. Then they entered the Temple together. The man was walking and jumping and praising God!

When I returned to the churches after my time at Duke, I was encouraged to try again to open eyes and spirits to this reality…God is still in the healing business. The Gospels, Matthew, Mark, Luke and John, tell us over and over Jesus healed the sick, the blind and the lame. The early Church did too. We are called to be Christ in the world. We have been honored to be able to be about the work that Jesus did! And Jesus said we would do greater things![40]

At prayer time one evening, Violet[41] came forward for prayer. "I wanted to come before tonight, but something kept holding me back. Pastor Patricia, I'm scared. I noticed Sunday I couldn't see much of anything in the Chancel area. My doctor has been treating my eyes, but my vision is much worse. I don't want to go blind. Please pray for me!" she said as her voice broke.

We laid hands on her and prayed. When we stopped, she looked up, "O Pastor! I can see everything in the Chancel area!! I can even read that plaque! O, thank you! Praise the Lord!!" She left with tears of joy.

The following Sunday, Jane came to me and asked, "Pastor, will you please pray for my shoulder? I slipped a few days ago and messed up my shoulder. The doctor said I needed surgery. I don't want to have surgery. It's scheduled for Tuesday."

---

[40] John 14:12

I motioned to a few of the Church leaders to join us in the room behind the Chancel. We laid hands on her and prayed. After some prayer, I asked, "How does your shoulder feel now?"

"Well, it's stopped hurting! Oh! I can raise it, and it doesn't hurt. Oh my! I have full rotation back! Praise the Lord!! It's healed!!"

One evening after Bible Study that focused on healing in the Book of Acts, John asked us to pray for his diabetes. All twelve of us gathered around him as we had with the others and prayed. He reported a few days later, he no longer needed insulin!

There were many healings: a man's gut looked precancerous, and after prayer, when his doctor checked him again, it was perfectly healthy. A leader at a retreat became ill and was better after we prayed. A young teacher attending healing prayer training needed prayer for a leg that was healed after prayer, and often there is inner healing of mind and spirit. We witnessed major back issues healed, a painful Baker's cyst in the back of a knee disappeared and more. At times healing follows spiritual or inner healing. This is the short list of healings I have witnessed. Beloved, again, God is REAL and present with us! Praise the Lord!

Chapter 22

God is Present to the End

I am with you always.

Matthew 28:20b *NIV*

A cherished story in our family was about the death of my Great-grandmother, Frances Jane. She lay dying for several days, and the family stayed by her side. Grandmother (we called her Mammaw) told me she was a woman of strong faith, and just before she died, she woke up and asked, "Oh, do you hear them? It's so beautiful! The angels are singing. You don't hear them?" Her tired expression changed to one of peace and joy. Soon after, she passed away peacefully.

Another Frances I met soon after moving to my first appointment shared her story about Jesus. She was 92 at that time. She began, "I was in my early thirties and had just given birth at the University of Virginia Hospital. There was a problem. I remember it was very black, like black velvet, and I was floating down and down when suddenly I stopped. Still couldn't see a thing. When a deep gravelly voice barked, 'Who are you? What are you doing here?' I told him I was Frances Hall. He barked back, 'You don't belong here! Get out of here!' As soon as he said this, I was flying up and up. At first, I saw a pinhole of light, and before I knew it, I was out in the light. It was beautiful, Pastor. Green rolling hills, I could see a beautiful city off in the distance and a road that led off toward that city. Then I noticed a man on the hill across from the one I was on and knew immediately it was Jesus. He was talking to two angels. Then they flew over and picked me up and carried me to him. Pastor, it was so beautiful there, so peaceful, and I could feel so much love. When I got to Jesus, he said, 'Frances, you have to go back.' "I don't want to go back! Please! I want to stay here with you! I begged."

"' No, Frances, you must go back. It's not your time.' Jesus said. Suddenly, I was back in the hospital bed with a sheet over my face. I pulled the sheet off, and almost immediately, a nurse came through the door and nearly fainted when she saw me. She murmured something and soon came back with the doctor. I asked them what happened. They wouldn't answer me. I told them I went to heaven, and Jesus sent me back. There was complete silence. So, I waited until no one was around and looked at the chart at the foot of my bed. There it was. The time of my death and the time the nurse found me alive again—about 40 minutes difference. O Pastor, I hope you can understand. I can't wait to go back there. Sometimes I just yearn to go. But I've tried to live a life that would please him."

Early in my career as a Pastor, I wondered where the "spiritual redwoods" were. To my joy, I found the first one. Frances was a "spiritual giant," and I was blessed to know her and hear her story. As long as she lived, she was one of our prayer warriors.

While still at this same appointment, I became a member of a pastor's support group. It was by invitation only. There were two Presbyterians, one Episcopalian, two Lutherans, one Baptist, and two Methodists pastors in the group. We shared each other's burdens, and being newly serving as a pastor, my time with these wonderful men and one other woman was a gift from heaven!

Michael[42] came in, almost walking on air. He was unusually energized! "What's with you today, Michael?" We asked.

---

[42] Name changed.

He responded, "I just came from the University Hospital, and the most incredible thing happened! I visited her yesterday, and we had a good visit about our time of transition from this life to the next. She said, 'I just don't want to be alone when my time comes.'"

He continued, "I believe strongly that the Lord sends angels to be with us at the end of life and shared that with her. She said she, too, really believed angels are all around us. I prayed she would be in the Lord's care and surrounded by angels and peace. This morning I went back to see her. Her bed was empty. A nurse came in and informed me that she had passed away several hours ago. 'I was just coming to strip her bed and make it fresh.' The nurse said. As she walked around to the other side of the bed, she bent over and picked up a large beautiful white feather. Then we both noticed there were two more! 'Where could these possibly have come from?' the nurse asked. 'We don't allow any feathers in the hospital.' Guys, I know the angels left them for me to find!"

I agree with him! Then I shared with them what a co-worker shared with me a few days after her sister died.

Jean seemed almost cheerful at such a time. Then she shared, "As you know, my sister and her fourteen-year-old son had moved in with us because we were to become his guardians, and my sister needed us at this time. Hospice has been wonderful. And after almost a month of being in a coma, we kept her son home that day because we knew her time was close. All of a sudden, she woke up, sat up in bed and stared across the room toward the corner. We asked her what she was looking at. She said, 'Don't you see him? It's Jesus.' Her face lit up, and she reached out and said, 'OK, I'm coming, Jesus.' And she laid back and died! Now who can be all down in the face after that?"

As strange or even morbid as it might sound to some, some of the most blessed moments of my life were in ministering to persons and families at the end of life. Those were moments when we were blessed and allowed to walk on Holy Ground.

No one knew Ellen[43] had a strong, beautiful voice. In her last days, we heard her singing, powerfully and beautifully, every word of some old, old hymns. Then she kept asking us to close the blind because the light coming from the window was too bright. There was no window where she pointed, and the blinds in the room were closed. This went on for several days. We all knew Ellen saw a glimpse of heaven.

In another experience, one of our members took her mother into their home in her last year. Ginny[44] had been in a coma for the last several visits. On this day, I mostly visited with our members and then suggested we go into Ginny's room for prayer.

I began my visit by saying, "Hello Ginny, it's Pastor Patricia. I thought we'd have a prayer with you."

"I know who you are." She surprised us. But she was not looking at me or her daughter. She was intent on something behind the two of us. "Look over there. There's Momma. And there's Joe." She pointed. She kept looking, and her lips were moving, but she was not voicing anything.

"She's seeing into heaven," I said gently to her daughter, who now was at the foot of the bed looking dumbfounded.

"She hasn't opened her eyes or said a word in two weeks!" her daughter exclaimed.

"Ginny, would you like for me to pray now?" I asked.

---

[43] Ditto
[44] Ditto.

"Yes, please," she said.

I do not remember what I prayed, and I learned that Ginny went on to a wonderful family reunion later that day.

So beloved, we are not alone even at the end of this journey. We hear angels sing, we are carried to Jesus by the angels, we see loved ones who have gone before us, and best of all, we see Jesus. We are never alone: we are always loved beyond our imaginations!

Conclusion

"We declare to you what we have seen and heard, so that you also may have fellowship with us; and truly our fellowship is with the Father and with his Son, Jesus Christ."
1 John 1:3 *NIV*

The above quote captures what I have tried to do in my writing. Henri J. M. Nouwen, writes in the *The Selfless Way of Christ:*

Thus, discipleship is the life of the Spirit in us, by whom we are lifted up into the divine life itself and receive new eyes to see, new ears to hear, and new hands to touch. Being lifted up in God's life, we are sent into the world to witness to what we have seen with our own eyes, have heard with our own ears, and have touched with our own hands.[45]

It is my prayer this has been accomplished!

---

[45] Nouwen, Henri J. M., Copyright 2012, Orbis Books, p. 43.

To The Reader

This has been a project scattered over many years. There were breaks because of illness, demands of ministry, moving, discouraging words of a friend and the internal spiritual struggle. There were times of just experiencing writer's block until old notes or journals were discovered in a box not yet opened. My struggle was whether it was now too late or too many personal memoirs. Does the Lord still want me to do this?

Then something would happen to renew my strength and determination to finish this work. Mark Batterson's books encouraged me greatly. Rereading and going back to those touchstone moments were also helpful and reaffirming that the Lord told me to do this. Much prayer has moved this work forward. There were times when the work of the enemy convinced me that I was to finish this work!

One day I opened the file on my computer, and only seven pages were there! When I last saw it, there were at least seventy-some pages! I panicked! When I was not writing, I was editing. I cannot begin to estimate how many hours of work that loss represented. There were additions that were not in the outline because they came to me after prayer or while editing, a memory would be triggered, and the memory was added only when I trusted the Lord provided the memory.

Then I remembered Dr. Francis MacNutt's sharing his struggle while writing one of his books, *Deliverance from Evil Spirits*. He was covered with much prayer. He had finished the book and had sent it to someone for editing. She pulled up the file, and she had a blank screen. Distraught, she called Francis and Judith MacNutt. They ran into her office, and all laid hands on the computer and prayed. The book, in its entirety, came back!

A few months ago, this book was, I felt, close to the finished product. Suddenly, the screen was white! Nothing was there! What a sinking feeling! But I laid my hands on the computer and prayed. I knew now that if God really wanted this book to be published, it would be restored in its entirety. It was! Thus, I am convinced it is to be, and I resolved to do whatever I can to see it published.

This was a work of love and to the glory of God!

Made in United States
North Haven, CT
30 September 2024